EZEKIEL
I Am the LORD

And so I will show My greatness and My holiness,
and I will make Myself known in the sight of many nations.
Then they will know that I am the LORD.
Ezekiel 38:23

Prepared from Materials Provided by Walter R. Roehrs

Revised Edition

CPH.
SAINT LOUIS

Project editor: Julene Gernant Dumit
Series editors: Thomas J. Doyle and Rodney L. Rathmann
Assistant to the editors: Cindi Crismon

We solicit your comments and suggestions concerning this material. Please write to Product Manager, Youth and Adult Bible Studies, Concordia Publishing House, 3558 South Jefferson Avenue, St. Louis, MO 63118-3968.

Contents

Preface

Welcome to the book of Ezekiel. You will find your study of this Old Testament prophecy particularly challenging and rewarding. Ezekiel is not an easy book. Among the prophets his style of presentation and use of symbolic language and images is most complex. For that reason we would suggest that groups undertaking this study be those who have met together for some time and have already done some study in the books of the New Testament as well as other portions of the Old Testament.

But in spite of its difficulty, Ezekiel's prophecy stands as a masterpiece of written revelation. The sense of awe and majesty in the words and visions of Ezekiel is among the most striking and inspiring in Scripture. And in this book you will discover again the central themes of judgment and deliverance as God deals with humanity. These themes are so crucial in the biblical revelation that they become the very key to the understanding of God's actions toward His human creatures. These themes are the central thrust of the Gospel of Jesus Christ as His life, death, and resurrection become the culmination of God's judgment upon sin and of His divine acts of rescue.

This booklet is a study guide. It is a tool to help you get into the book of Ezekiel, to work through the message there, to relate the meaning of the revelation to your own life and your own concerns. It is a book designed to help you study this Word of God and share your insights with other Christians. This booklet is not a verse-by-verse commentary on the book; it does not attempt a complete theological analysis of the prophet's message. You are encouraged to use Bible dictionaries, Bible helps, study Bibles, and commentaries to enrich your study. Read them before class, bring them to class to refer to, and use them in private study to gain insights that you can share with the whole class.

Be alert to how Ezekiel points forward to Christ and His kingdom. Referring to the Old Testament, Jesus said, "The Scriptures ... testify about Me" **(John 5:39)**. All of us need to hear God's Word speak to us of our need for a Savior and to rejoice at the proclamation of the Good News of salvation in Jesus Christ.

May God bless you as you study. May His Spirit work through God's Word to strengthen your faith and to help you to rededicate yourselves to lives of love and service.

Lesson 1

The Glory of the Lord (Ezekiel 1)

Theme Verse

"The heavens were opened and I saw visions of God" **(Ezekiel 1:1).**

Goal

We seek to understand Ezekiel's vision of the living creatures and the glory of the Lord and how that vision would have brought comfort to the exiles in Babylon.

What's Going On Here?

Begin your class by reading the following material aloud: It was July 593 B.C. A little over four years earlier (April 597) Nebuchadnezzar had carried off the upper strata of the chosen people to Babylonia **(2 Kings 24:10–16).** Here some of them were settled at Tel Abib on the Kebar River, a canal of the Euphrates River. To the exiles the world seemed out of joint. The heavens no longer were declaring the glory of God **(Psalm 19:1).** Instead they seemed to proclaim His defeat. His loss of control appeared complete when a few years later the holy city and His temple were leveled **(2 Kings 25:8–12).** All the stars of hope and salvation, promised to all nations through the offspring of Abraham, were eclipsed by the glaring brilliance of brutal forces of evil.

Into this world of dark despair, the glory of the Lord suddenly burst with such blinding light and such cosmic configurations as to rouse even the most dispirited from their stupor of doubt and to strike terror into all who defied Him. He was not an idol locked up in the walls of a shrine. In the very heartland of the conqueror, the heavens were opened to assert His worldwide dominion.

One of the captives, Ezekiel a priest, the son of Buzi, was permitted to see visions of God. It was to solve the riddle of his life and that of his fellow exiles. What he saw was so out of this world that he was constrained to say its features were "like" some mundane phenomena or had their "appearance." For he beheld

- a fiery storm cloud, coming from the north out of which emerged
- four unearthly creatures propelling
- a four-wheeled chariot bearing
- a celestial platform on which was enthroned
- the glory of the Lord, framed by
- the bright colors of the rainbow.

Overwhelmed by the vision, Ezekiel fell upon his face. Yet its basic meaning could not escape him. He was made aware of the Lord's dominion over everything in His created universe. All creatures, whether inanimate or animate, are at His beck and call as He shapes world history.

Read **Ezekiel 1** aloud. Try to capture the awesomeness of the vision. What does the vision say to you about God? What do you think it said to Ezekiel? to the people of his day?

Searching the Scriptures

If we bear in mind that the vision appeared in the land of Israel's captors, it may help to explain some of its features. Read **Ezekiel 1** again. Then concentrate on some of these specifics. You might assign each of the following references to a small group for discussion and then share insights after a few minutes.

1. **Verse 4**—*North.* The Babylonians thought of the north as the primordial home of the gods. How did the Hebrew people view it differently based on the words of **Jeremiah** in **1:14** and **4:6?**

2. **Verse 4**—*A stormy wind and a cloud.* The captives heard the Babylonians praise their chief god Marduk as "the Lord of the storm." See **Nahum 1:3**. What do **Ezekiel** and **Nahum** reveal about the stormy wind?

3. **Verse 13**—*Fire.* Would the god Marduk enable the Babylonians to burn Jerusalem and the temple? No! What assurance for the exiles do you find in **Deuteronomy 4:24** and **Isaiah 10:17?** Compare also **Ezekiel 10:2.**

4. **Verse 26**—*Throne.* Marduk occupied the throne of the Babylonian pantheon. What could the exiles have remembered from **Isaiah 6:1** and **1 Kings 22:19?** How would that memory have helped them?

5. **Verses 15–19**—*A wheel within a wheel.* A statue of Marduk was paraded through the streets of Babylon in ornate vehicles. The celestial chariot at the Lord's command had four bisecting wheels and was therefore ready to proceed in all directions without turning. How might these words of Ezekiel have reminded Israel of what happened in **2 Kings 2:11?** See also **Habakkuk 3:8**. What comfort would they have found?

6. **Verses 5–14**—*Living creatures.* The exiles heard the Babylonians assign magical powers to grotesque beings, depicted and sculptured with combined human and animal features. Israel was to be reminded that the Creator had agents at His disposal who represented different kinds of earthly beings animated by the breath of life. In **10:1** Ezekiel called them cherubim. In what place known to all Israelites were two golden cherubim found **(Exodus 25:17–22)?** Because of this, how was the Lord often described **(1 Samuel 4:4; Isaiah 37:16; Psalm 99:1)?**

7. **Verse 18**—*Full of eyes.* Bizarre in our world where the animate and the inanimate are separate categories, this feature of the celestial vehicle would seem to indicate that it could see and avoid obstacles in its path. Compare **Revelation 4:6–8.** How would you interpret this feature?

8. **Verse 26**—*A figure like that of a man.* Ezekiel was careful not to say that he saw God directly or to imply that the infinite God could be confined to a human body. Why (see **Exodus 33:20** and **1 Timothy 6:15–16)?**

9. **Verse 28**—*The glory of the Lord.* What Ezekiel did see was "the appearance of the likeness of the glory of the LORD" **(v. 28).** In the past, the glory of the Lord had sometimes been visible in the form of a cloud and/or a brilliant light. This was the sign of God's presence among His people. Read **Exodus 40:34–38** and **1 Kings 8:6–11.** Where was the usual dwelling place of the Lord's glory? What comfort would it have been to the exiles to know that the Lord's glory had appeared to Ezekiel in a land far from that usual dwelling place?

10. **Verse 28**—*A rainbow.* The windstorm and the immense cloud of **verse 4** foreboded disaster. However, beyond and above the threatened darkness of judgment, the divine light of forgiving mercy continued to shine as brightly as before. How would **Genesis 9:12–16** have helped the Israelites focus on the mercy of God?

The Word for Us

1. Ezekiel saw visions of God, but he did not see God face to face. Only one person has ever done that. Read **John 1:18; 14:6–10.** Who is that person? Of what benefit is that to us?

2. New Age philosophy, based in part on Eastern religious practice, promotes various exercises and manipulations that claim to bring about the merging of human consciousness with a universal, transcendent world-spirit. How does God's revelation to Ezekiel differ from such self-induced attempts to rise above our world of senses?

3. Read **Revelation 4.** How was John's vision like Ezekiel's? How was it different? Recall that John was writing to people under persecution. How are the messages alike? What meaning do these messages have for us today?

4. Talk about situations today in which Ezekiel's vision might be helpful.

Closing

Sing or speak together the following stanzas of "Immortal, Invisible, God Only Wise."

Immortal, invisible, God only wise,
In light inaccessible hid from our eyes,
Most blessed, most glorious, O Ancient of Days,
Almighty, victorious, Your great name we praise!

Great Father of glory, pure Father of light,
Your angels adore You, enveiling their sight.
All laud we would render; oh, lead us to see
The light of Your splendor, Your love's majesty!

To Do This Week

Read **Ezekiel 2–3.**

Lesson 2

A Watchman
(Ezekiel 2–3)

Theme Verse

"Son of man, I have made you a watchman for the house of Israel; so hear the word I speak and give them warning from Me" (Ezekiel 3:17).

Goal

We seek to understand Ezekiel's call to be a spiritual watchman for the people of Israel and the characteristics of the word that He spoke.

What's Going On Here?

Read Ezekiel 2–3 silently or ask volunteers to read portions aloud. Then read this material to aid your understanding. Discuss questions that may arise.

Ezekiel was not to be a holy man basking in the afterglow of his vision, spending his time in private meditation. The Spirit put him on his feet because God had work for him to do. It would not be an easy task. He was to go to a rebellious house. His hearers would react to the word he was to bring them like briers and thorns and scorpions (2:6). Furthermore, the message assigned to him might not be to his liking, for it contained "words of lament and mourning and woe" (2:10). In the end, however, these bitter words would become as sweet as honey in Ezekiel's mouth (3:3).

He was to know in advance too that he would not have an easy time of it because he was not being sent to a people of foreign speech but to the house of Israel (3:5), people who spoke his own language. The people to whom he spoke would understand the sound of his words, but in their hardness and obstinacy (3:7), they would be impervious to the intended effect of his words on their conscience and will. Though promised to be equipped against their insolence with a mental and spiritual fortitude "harder than flint" (3:9), Ezekiel "went in bitterness and in the anger of [his] spirit" (3:14) to the exiles and "sat among them for seven days—overwhelmed" (3:15). In order to overcome his natural disinclination to assume his assignment, "the strong hand of the LORD" was upon him (3:14).

Ezekiel was not, like Moses, to play the role of a national hero and lead an enslaved people to freedom. Yet his message was to have crucial results for his hearers. It was a matter of life and death that they hear what he had to say. For like a watchman doing sentinel duty on a city's ramparts, he was to send out bugle calls to alert the people of danger to their lives. If he failed to sound a clear and unambiguous warning, his own life would be forfeited. But having done so, he would not be held accountable for anyone's refusal to turn from his or her wicked way (3:19).

In a final directive Ezekiel was told that, for a specific time, he would not be able to "go out among the people" (3:25) and talk about general topics of interest or even reprove them in words of his own choosing. The Lord would cause him to be dumb except when the Lord provided him with the message he was to deliver.

Apparently to prepare and fortify the newly commissioned prophet for his arduous task, the vision of God's glory, which he had seen by the Kebar River appeared to him again (3:23).

Searching the Scriptures

1. In 2:1 Ezekiel is not addressed by his name, but as "Son of man." This phrase, which could also be translated "Son of Adam," is used 93 times in **Ezekiel.** It is a reminder to Ezekiel of his humanity. Why might such a reminder have been important?

The word that Ezekiel preached was remarkable, multifaceted, and effective. Let's look at some of the characteristics of the prophetic word.

2. *A word that cannot be silenced* (**2:3–7**). How does **Ezekiel 33:21** support the conviction that nothing could nullify the inspired message of impending judgment uttered by Ezekiel?

3. *A bitter word that becomes sweet* (**2:8–3:3**). In a visionary experience Ezekiel ate a scroll inscribed with a distasteful message of judgment. Having eaten it, Ezekiel found that it tasted sweet. Compare **Jeremiah 15:16** and **Revelation 10:8–10.** What similarities and differences do you see? What is said about the task of the prophet in each case? How might the experience of proclaiming the Word be similar today?

4. *A word transforming weakness into strength* (**3:4–11**). Strengthened by God and armed with His word, Ezekiel would not flinch from confronting stubborn hearts, whether they listened or refused to listen. Compare **2 Corinthians 12:7–10.** How was Paul's experience similar to Ezekiel's? What does Paul's experience say to us?

5. *A word that overwhelms* **(3:12–15).** Not a puppet or automaton, when the hand of the Lord was upon him, it is likely that Ezekiel had to overcome his own inclination to refuse his assignment, as did other spokesmen of God. Compare **Exodus 3:11; Jonah 1:1–3; Jeremiah 1:4–6.** What similarities do you see? What does the comparison say about God's choosing and those whom He chooses? Relate your findings to Paul's experience in **Acts 9:1–9.**

6. *A word of responsibility* **(3:16–21).** As watchman, Ezekiel had a position of grave responsibility. Compare **Ezekiel 33:1–6** and **Hebrews 13:17.** What is a watchman responsible for? What is he not responsible for? How does the responsibility make the pastoral office more difficult? Why is the message of forgiveness important to professional church workers too?

7. *An exclusive word* **(3:22–27).** It dare never be diluted with human opinions or toned down to satisfy objections of the old Adam. Compare **Deuteronomy 4:2** and **Revelation 22:18–19.** What is our responsibility

when we speak God's truth? What part of God's revelation is most difficult for you to talk about? Why? How can we help one another in our witness to Jesus?

The Word for Us

1. In order to come to life and to espouse God's cause, Ezekiel needed the Spirit to infuse vitalizing energy into his inert body **(2:1–2),** much as the lifeless clay of Adam became a living being only after God "breathed into his nostrils the breath of life" **(Genesis 2:7).** What was necessary for us to become spiritually alive according to **Ephesians 2:1–10?** What is the result of that coming to life for us? How is our living task similar to Ezekiel's **(Ephesians 2:10)?**

2. In what sense are we "prophets" today? How is our task as witnesses different from Ezekiel's? What word of judgment do we have to speak? What word of grace, of forgiveness?

Closing

Ask the blessing of God on the ministry of your spiritual leaders and on your task as witnesses by singing or reading together the following stanzas of "Lord of the Living Harvest."

Lord of the living harvest
That whitens on the plain,
Where angels soon shall gather
Their sheaves of golden grain,
Accept these hands to labor,
These hearts to trust and love,
And with them ever hasten
Your kingdom from above.

Be with them, God the Father,
Be with them, God the Son
And God the Holy Spirit,
Most blessed Three in One.
Teach them, as faithful servants
You rightly to adore,
And fill them with Your fullness
Both now and evermore.

To Do This Week

Read **Ezekiel 4–5.**

Lesson 3

A Sign for Israel (Ezekiel 4–5)

Theme Verse

"Therefore this is what the Sovereign LORD says: I Myself am against you, Jerusalem, and I will inflict punishment on you in the sight of the nations" **(Ezekiel 5:8)**.

Goal

We seek to understand the message of judgment that Ezekiel proclaimed to God's rebellious people, the symbolic method he used to do so, and the hope that would remain when God's fury was spent.

What's Going On Here?

In many cases Ezekiel not only spoke for God but actually acted out His message. In these chapters we have a series of these action sermons.

Ezekiel transmitted what he heard with his ears and received with his heart **(3:10)** by acting out the entrusted message in four pantomimes. We will look at each individually.

Searching the Scriptures

Before studying each of the symbolic acts however, let us look at the medium of symbolic acts in general. Ezekiel was not involved in playful charades performed to entertain an audience, nor was he doing tricks of voodoo-like magic, automatically effecting desired results. The prophet was not a witch doctor.

1. What did God say about occult and superstitious practices in **Ezekiel 13:17–23?** See also **Exodus 22:18; Leviticus 20:27; Deuteronomy 18:9–14.**

2. At God's command Ezekiel communicated visually what he also proclaimed by word of mouth. Does **Ezekiel 3:7** give a clue why Ezekiel was called to engage in more symbolic actions than other prophets?

3. Look at how Isaiah and Jeremiah acted out messages according to **Isaiah 20:2–4** and **Jeremiah 13:1–11.** In what way was the purpose of their acts similar to or different from Ezekiel's? Compare **Acts 21:10–14.**

Now let's look at the symbolic acts themselves. Select a volunteer to read **Ezekiel 4:1–3** aloud. Then read the following paragraph.

In the first symbolic act, Ezekiel put to rest the false notion held by some that God would never demean Himself by destroying Jerusalem, the place where His glory dwelt. To set them right, Ezekiel took a soft clay tablet and on it sketched the city of Jerusalem in a state of siege. As a sign that God would not intervene and lift the siege, he placed an iron pan between the besieged city and himself, God's representative. No cry for deliverance from the besieged city would penetrate the ironclad decree of the city's destruction. The enemy would press the siege to its bitter end.

Now read **Ezekiel 4:4–8** and the following paragraphs.

In his second dramatized sermon, Ezekiel made clear to the rebellious house that its threatened doom was not a chance happening or an accident of history. God had decreed it, and He had every reason to inflict it. Both Israel, the 10 northern tribes, and Judah, the Southern Kingdom, had kindled the wrath of God by their wickedness and idolatry and had to bear their punishment. Note that the punishment of the Northern Kingdom of Israel had already begun. Many of its people had been carried into captivity by the Assyrians over 120 years earlier.

In acting out the reason for the divine decree, Ezekiel played the role of the apostate people. As if crushed to the ground by a heavy burden and held by ropes to prevent escape, he lay on his left side and then on his right side for a specified number of days, representatively bearing the sins of the people. Ezekiel was not bearing the punishment for the sins of the people but figuratively representing them.

The large number of days Ezekiel was required to lie on his left and on his right side symbolized either the number of years that the people had sinned or the number of years that they would be punished. In addition, it is hard for us to know whether actual, chronological years were meant and if so which ones or whether these were figurative numbers, denoting a long time. Most likely the symbolism was clearer to Ezekiel and his audience.

4. Read **Exodus 12:40.** What might the total number of Ezekiel's symbolic act have called to mind for the people of Israel?

5. It is likely that Ezekiel lay on his side long enough each day to teach the intended lesson. How do you think his message was received? How would his foretelling of judgment be received today? How would the accusations of unfaithfulness and idolatry fit our world?

Read **Ezekiel 4:9–17** aloud. Then read this paragraph:

A third series of symbolic actions was to simulate the physical and spiritual anguish the rebellious house would endure during the siege and the ensuing exile. Portraying the coming lack of bread and water, Ezekiel was to eat a daily ration of bread,weighing no more than eight ounces (0.2 kilogram), and to drink no more than about two-thirds quart (0.6 liter) of water.

6. The siege of Jerusalem would necessitate severe rationing of food and water. How desperate did conditions finally become according to **Lamentations 1:11; 2:11–12, 20; 4:4, 10?**

The dough for Ezekiel's bread, made from an assortment of coarse grains, was to be baked over a fire fueled by human dung. This was to depict the ritual uncleanness that the people would not be able to avoid during the siege and the exile.

7. How did Ezekiel react to the Lord's instructions? Why (see **Leviticus 22:8; Deuteronomy 23:12–14**)? How was Ezekiel allowed to avoid defilement?

Read **Ezekiel 5:1–17** and these paragraphs:

The dramatized threat of Israel's doom reached a climax in a fourth series of symbolic actions. They portrayed how furious the Lord's chastisements of the faithless people would be.

The paraphernalia to be used in this deadly object lesson were (1) a sharp sword, honed to a razor's edge; (2) the prophet's hair, cut and shaved from his head and beard; (3) a set of scales to weigh the hair and to divide it into three heaps, the first to be burned, the second to be struck with the sword, the third to be scattered to the wind; (4) the folds of the prophet's robe, into which a few strands of hair were to be placed.

8. Ezekiel, acting as God's representative, was to smite, burn, and scatter the hair of his head and beard. Of what was it a sign if a man shaved his hair according to **Jeremiah 48:37–38** and **Isaiah 15:2–3?** What would the picture of Ezekiel's shaved hair say to the people?

9. God had made Israel the center of the nations **(5:5),** not in a geographic sense but to be the focal point from which humanity's salvation was to radiate to the ends of the earth. What had the people done with their chosen position and their calling according to **5:6–7, 11?**

10. What was the Lord's response to the people's unfaithfulness **(5:8–12, 14–17)?** What were Ezekiel's actions with his hair meant to symbolize?

11. This almost unremittingly gloomy picture of judgment still had a ray of hope. According to **Ezekiel 6:8,** what was the hope for those represented by the few strands of hair preserved in Ezekiel's garment?

12. When the destruction was finished and the Lord's fury was spent, what would the survivors, often called the remnant, know and do **(5:13; 6:8–10)?**

The Word for Us

1. Some say that the God of the Old Testament is a vicious, arbitrary ruler given to violent bursts of passion. People who would rather picture God as a kind of Santa in the sky find God's judgment repulsive. What is your picture of God? How do you deal with God's judgment? What does God's judgment say to you? What did John the Baptist say about the wrath of God in **Matthew 3:7–12?** What did Jesus say about it in **Matthew 25:41?** How does the knowledge of the judgment of God prepare us for the Good News of salvation in Jesus Christ?

2. We live in a culture where logic more than figurative language is used to convey information. We most often use figurative language only to illustrate a point rather than to make it. Biblical culture was much different in this respect. The prophets and Jesus often used word pictures and parables to convey messages. How might our communication be enhanced if we took the time to construct word pictures to convey our meaning? Can you think of a situation in which the message was more effectively communicated using an analogy or word picture than a logical explanation? What uses might this type of communication have as we share God's Law and Gospel with others?

Closing

Pray together:

O Lord, we know that Your wrath against sin is real. We know that we are sinners and deserve nothing but Your wrath. We have been unfaithful to You in our thoughts, words, and actions. Lord, we are sincerely sorry for our sins, and we ask for Your forgiveness for Jesus' sake and for the power of Your Holy Spirit to amend our sinful lives. We pray trusting in Your mercy. Amen.

To Do This Week

Read **Ezekiel 6–7.**

Lesson 4

The Day of Doom
(Ezekiel 6–7)

Theme Verse

"Son of man, this is what the Sovereign LORD says to the land of Israel: The end! The end has come upon the four corners of the land" **(Ezekiel 7:2).**

Goal

We aim to understand Ezekiel's words of judgment against the entire nation of Judah and why God was sending that judgment as well as how God felt about it.

What's Going On Here?

The pronouncement of judgment and doom continues with deadening repetition. The gloom is almost complete. While the last two chapters focused on the judgment that was to befall Jerusalem, these chapters tell of the disaster coming on the entire land, from north to south, and the reasons for it.

Searching the Scriptures

Before we look in depth at **Ezekiel 6–7,** let's look at two phrases that we will find repeatedly throughout **Ezekiel.**

1. How did Ezekiel often introduce a new revelation from the Lord that he was to speak **(6:1; 7:1)?** What did this emphasize about his message?

The second phrase, "the Sovereign LORD," is the NIV translation of "the Lord (Adonai) Yahweh." *Yahweh* is God's personal name, the name that He revealed to Moses at the burning bush **(Exodus 3:13–15).** As do many translations, the NIV uses "the LORD" (with capital letters) to translate *Yahweh.* The Hebrew word *Adonai* is usually translated "the Lord" (without all capitals). But when the two words occur together, it would be awkward to translate them as "the Lord the LORD," so the NIV translators chose the phrase *the Sovereign Lord.*

2. Read **Ezekiel 6.** Ezekiel was to set his face (either literally or figuratively in opposition) toward the mountains of Israel where abundant and undeniable evidence of the nation's guilt was in plain view, demonstrating the justice of its punishment. The high places mentioned in **6:3,** Canaanite in origin, were local cult sites. They were usually but not always located on geographical heights. What was Israel commanded in **Deuteronomy 12:1–6?** Why do you think this was commanded?

But many Israelites were not very zealous in following the commands given in **Deuteronomy 12.** Throughout their history pagan worship sites were a snare to them. In such places people often blatantly worshiped idols and/or succumbed to these temptations: to use pagan worship practices such as sacred prostitution to worship Yahweh; to assign ideas about idols to Yahweh; to think that Yahweh was only one among many gods. Time and time again pagan practices and ideas were condemned by the prophets, and righteous kings attempted to wipe them out. But all these efforts were to no lasting avail.

3. It was not only on hilltops that abominable practices occurred. Abhorrent things also went on in ravines and valleys. What was done in one valley according to **Jeremiah 19:1–6?**

4. What would the Lord do to these worship sites and the people who worshiped there **(6:3–6, 11–13)**?

5. How complete would the destruction be **(6:6, 14)**?

6. By worshiping idols and corrupting the worship of Yahweh with pagan practices and ideas, the people were denying the Lordship of Yahweh. When the destruction was finished, what would the survivors know **(6:7, 10, 13–14)**? Be alert for this phrase throughout **Ezekiel;** you will find it many times.

7. Reread **6:8–10.** Even in the midst of His fierce anger, the Lord's justice was tempered by mercy. There would be survivors for the fulfillment of God's promise, a remnant for whom and through whom God's plan of salvation in Christ would come to pass. In exile, what would these survivors remember about the Lord? How would they feel about themselves and their actions?

8. How was the image of destruction in **6:5** picked up and made different in **37:1–14**? How did this promise of restoration begin to go into effect according to **Ezra 1:1–4?**

9. Read **7:1–14.** In order to dispel the entrenched delusion that the holy city and the temple could not be destroyed, Ezekiel composed his message in yet another form. As if attending the nation's funeral, he broke out into a frenzied lament over its death, repeating the doleful word *end* in brief staccato-like refrains, the style of which is hard to capture in English. How often does the word occur in these verses? In order to drive home the point that the day of mourning cannot be deflected, he punctuates the dirge with the words *come* or *coming*. How often? The day of God's patience and forbearance with the nation, guilty of abominations, had passed. Read the verses again aloud. Read them as they might be cried or called at a funeral. What is the feeling of the words? What might have been the impact of such a funeral-like lament on the hearers?

10. Read **7:15–22.** The people would be struck with terror and filled with shame because of their sins. They would long to fill their stomachs, but the only available things would be the silver and gold that they had so treasured. These things would be useless in the absence of food. Compare **7:22** with **Numbers 6:22–27.** What would God do? What do the words used to describe the temple say about how God feels about the coming destruction?

11. Read **7:23–27. Ezekiel 7:23** depicts reasons in addition to idolatry for the coming judgment. What are they? How would God deal with the people **(7:27)?**

12. Jeremiah prophesied during roughly the same time period as Ezekiel, only Jeremiah was not taken into exile. Contrary to what Jeremiah said, what did his contemporaries assume about their civil and religious leadership (see **Jeremiah 18:18**)? What in fact would happen to their leadership according to **Ezekiel 7:26–27?**

The Word for Us

1. Few people bow down to physical statues today, but idolatry is alive and well. Read aloud Luther's definition of a god:

> A god is that to which we look for all good and in which we find refuge in every time of need. To have a god is nothing else than to trust and believe him with our whole heart. As I have often said, the trust and faith of the heart alone make both God and an idol. If your faith and trust are right, then your God is the true God. On the other hand, if your trust is false and wrong, then you have not the true God. For these two belong together, faith and God. That to which your heart clings and entrusts itself is, I say, really your God (Large Catechism I 2–3, *The Book of Concord*, ed. Theodore G. Tappert [Fortress Press, 1959]).

List some of the things that people make into their gods today. How might you help someone whose god is not the true God see the unreliability of that in which he or she trusts?

2. As long as all was going well for the idolatrous people of Israel, they were content in their unfaithfulness to God. It took the exile to awaken them to the fact that Yahweh is the Lord. In what way might trouble lead people today (believers and unbelievers) to acknowledge the rule of God? How is it possible for trouble to have the opposite result? How does serious trouble usually affect your relationship to God?

Closing

Sing or read together "Christians, While on Earth Abiding."

Christians, while on earth abiding,
Let us never cease to pray,
Firmly in the Lord confiding
As our parents in their day.
Be the children's voices raised
To the God their parents praised.
May His blessing, failing never,
Rest upon His people ever.

Bless us, Father, and protect us
From all harm in all our ways;
Patiently, O Lord, direct us
Safely through these fleeting days.
Let Your face upon us shine,
Fill us with Your peace divine.
Praise the Father, Son, and Spirit!
Praise Him, all who life inherit!

To Do This Week

Read **Ezekiel 8–9.**

Lesson 5

Visions of Crime and Punishment (Ezekiel 8–9)

Theme Verse

"He stretched out what looked like a hand and took me by the hair of my head. The Spirit lifted me up between earth and heaven and in visions of God He took me to Jerusalem, to the entrance to the north gate of the inner court, where the idol that provokes to jealousy stood" **(Ezekiel 8:3)**.

Goal

We aim to understand the idolatry that provoked the Lord to jealousy and anger and rejoice in the fact that He would preserve those who had remained faithful to Him.

What's Going On Here?

Up to this point in the book, Ezekiel has participated in a dramatic vision of the heavenly throne **(chapters 1–3)** and has proclaimed the judgment of God to the people through symbolic acts **(chapters 4–5)** and through the spoken word **(chapters 6–7)**.

Now the scene dramatically shifts again. We return to a vision, but this time a vision that includes the themes of judgment and salvation that have been presented in the preceding chapters.

These chapters have the characteristics of a kind of trial. In **chapter 8** the evidence of faithlessness and idolatry was amassed before the prophet, who saw it all from God's point of view in a transported vision. In **chapter 9** the sentence was given and carried out by visionary figures in a way that told of the severity of God's judgment and His desire to save those who were faithful.

Searching the Scriptures

Read **8:1–6.** Fourteen months after his first vision, Ezekiel was sitting in his house, evidently being consulted by the elders of Judah. There Ezekiel saw a figure who had the same description as the figure he saw on the throne in his first vision. Reluctant to describe the Lord in human terms, Ezekiel said that this figure stretched out what *looked like* a hand and took him by the hair. In a trance-like experience (not physically), Ezekiel was transported by the Spirit to the temple in Jerusalem. There, at the entrance to the north gate between the inner and outer courts, Ezekiel was shown something that belonged in the temple and something that did not.

1. What did Ezekiel see **(8:4–5)**?

2. Why did this idol provoke the Lord to jealousy (see **Exodus 20:3–5**)? Compare **2 Kings 21:1–7.**

3. What would be the result of such detestable practices **(Ezekiel 8:6)**?

Read **8:7–13.** The veneration of animals, including crocodiles, snakes, and bugs, was prevalent in Egypt. Imported to Jerusalem, it apparently was practiced in secret. Ezekiel had some trouble finding the door to the chamber where 70 elders were burning incense to the idols engraved all over the walls. Read **Exodus 20:4–6.**

4. Why would the sin recounted here in **Ezekiel** be particularly grievous according to the **Exodus** passage?

5. What did the elders assume about the Lord **(Ezekiel 8:12)?** What characteristics of the Lord were they denying by those assumptions?

Read **8:14–15.** Worshiped widely from Babylonia to Asia Minor, this idol is mentioned by name only here in the Old Testament. He was thought to embody the power to activate and sustain the processes of vegetation. When plant life disappeared in fall and winter, he was said to have died. Women sat weeping over his death as a propitiatory rite to promote his revival in spring, when the rain would again vitalize the dormant soil.

6. Suppose you were a child of Israel and knew such teachings as those in **Genesis 1:9–13; 8:22; Jeremiah 5:22–24; Job 38:1–7, 22–30;** and especially **Exodus 20:3.** Why would the worship of Tammuz be a particular abomination?

Read **8:16–18.** In a final scene of idolatrous practice, Israel's abominations reached a climax. The priests who were to teach the law deliberately broke it. They turned their backs on the temple of the Lord and worshiped the sun.

When the priests put the branch to their nose, they engaged in a cultic act which remains unexplained. In any case, their idolatry was extreme. To the people who worshiped the God who "created the heavens and the earth" **(Genesis 1:1),** the worship of heavenly bodies was particularly abhorrent, though it was common in the ancient world.

7. See **Deuteronomy 4:19.** What had the Lord said to His people about the heavenly bodies?

As if these detestable practices were not enough, the people also filled the land with violence and constantly provoked the Lord's anger. In anger and without pity, He would deal with them. The coming judgment would be graphically visualized for Ezekiel in the coming chapters.

Read **9:1–11.** The six angelic executioners, summoned to smite the citizens of Jerusalem with their weapons for slaughter, give a dramatic exhibition of the principle that God will deal in anger **(8:18)** with those whose guilt is exceedingly great.

8. What preceded the Lord's directions to the messengers He had summoned **(9:3)?**

9. The executioners were to touch no one upon whom was the mark made on their foreheads by a seventh man. Sparing those who grieved over the abominations gave a visual demonstration of what divine principle **(18:4)?**

10. The angelic servant who carried out the order was clothed in linen, as were others acting as God's representatives or on His behalf (see **Exodus 28:42–43; 1 Samuel 2:18; Daniel 10:5; Revelation 19:14**). What does linen symbolize in **Revelation 19:7–8?**

11. Who will have a mark or seal on their forehead according to **Revelation 7:3; 9:4; 14:1; 22:3–4?** What does the mark mean? From what will it protect those who bear it?

12. What role did Ezekiel play in **Ezekiel 9:8?** What was the Lord's response **(9:9–10)?**

13. On what note of hope does the chapter end **(9:11)?**

The Word for Us

1. What do **Isaiah 1:2–4; 44:12–17; Jeremiah 2:13; 17:13;** and **Romans 1:18–25** say to those who think they can turn their backs on God boldly or in secret and get away with it because God does not really care? What warning is here for us?

2. We have a remnant of sun worship in astrology. What danger is there in even a casual use of horoscopes and readings? What would you say to those who trust in them?

3. As noted in the last lesson, idolatry is pervasive yet today. What forms of idolatry are warned against in **Matthew 6:24** and **Philippians 3:19?** What kinds of idolatry most often tempt you? What helps you in times when something or someone takes God's place in your life? What help can you offer to other Christians who struggle with the same temptations? From where does the strength to remain faithful to the Lord come (see **Philippians 1:4–6**)?

Closing

Sing or read together the following stanzas of "From God Can Nothing Move Me."

From God can nothing move me;
He will not step aside
But always will reprove me
And be my constant guide.
He stretches out His hand
In evening and in morning,
Providing His forewarning
Wherever I may stand.

When those whom I regarded
As trustworthy and sure
Have long from me departed,
God's grace shall still endure.
He cares for all my needs,
From sin and shame corrects me,
From Satan's bonds protects me;
Not even death succeeds.

To Do This Week

Read **Ezekiel 10–11.**

Lesson 6

Jerusalem Burned and Forsaken (Ezekiel 10–11)

Theme Verse

"The glory of the LORD went up from within the city and stopped above the mountain east of it" **(Ezekiel 11:23).**

Goal

We seek to understand the remainder of Ezekiel's vision of the Lord's glory departing from Jerusalem and His promise to be with His faithful remnant and return them to the land of Israel.

What's Going On Here?

These chapters record the continuation of the vision begun in **Ezekiel 8.** Having been brought in visions of God to Jerusalem, Ezekiel now saw the prophetic threat of the end actualized before him. The holy city, its inhabitants slaughtered **(chapter 9),** was put to the torch and deserted by the Lord.

Searching the Scriptures

Read **Ezekiel 10:1–8.** The movement of the glory of the Lord is somewhat unclear in this section. **Ezekiel 10:4** could be translated "The glory of the LORD had risen. ..." In that case, it would be a restatement of the movement of the glory noted in **9:3.** (See the answer to question 8 of the previous lesson.) Perhaps Ezekiel wanted to emphasize that the glory was still in same position by the threshold.

1. What did the Lord command the man in linen, the angel of mercy from **chapter 9 (10:2)?** How was the prophecy fulfilled according to **2 Kings 25:8–9?** What did Ezekiel's vision say about whose agents the Babylonians were?

Read **Ezekiel 10:9–17.** Ezekiel turned his attention to a description of the cherubim. He noted particularly their mobility and that of the four wheels beside them. Ezekiel also noted that these bearers of the Lord's glory were the living creatures that he had seen by the Kebar River (**chapter 1**). It is unclear why one of the faces is here described as that of a cherub, whereas in **chapter 1** it was described as the face of an ox.

2. Read **Ezekiel 10:18–22.** Recount the movement of the glory of the Lord. What is the temple called in **10:19?**

3. Read **Jeremiah 7:1–15.** What mistaken notion did the people have about the temple? How did both Jeremiah and Ezekiel seek to dispel that notion?

Read **Ezekiel 11:1–4.** In his vision Ezekiel also was taken to the east gate of the temple. There he saw 25 leaders of the people. Two of them are named but are otherwise not known from Scripture. These leaders were giving deceptive advice to the people. The meaning of their words concerning the building of houses is somewhat unclear. It could be that they were advising people that the city was in no danger and soon it would be time to build houses (a peace-time activity). Or perhaps they were saying that people should not build houses but should concentrate their efforts on shoring up the city's defenses (ignoring Jeremiah's warning that those who resisted the Babylonians would die [Jeremiah 21:8–10]). These leaders considered those left in the city to be the choice pieces of meat who were protected inside the pot—the city. Ezekiel was commanded to prophesy against these leaders.

4. Read **Ezekiel 11:5–12.** What did the Spirit of the Lord lead Ezekiel to say?

Read **11:13.** As if to confirm what Ezekiel was prophesying, one of the leaders fell dead as Ezekiel was speaking. Perhaps the man actually died in Jerusalem at that moment, and Ezekiel saw it in his vision. Or Ezekiel's vision was a prophecy of his later death.

Pelatiah's death and the prospect of a massacre of the people in Jerusalem terrified Ezekiel. Was God about to make a complete end of the remnant of Israel, leaving none to be the bearers of the promise made to Abraham and his descendants?

Read **11:14–15.** In response to Ezekiel's question, the Lord quoted what the people of Jerusalem were saying—that those who had already been taken into exile were far from the Lord and that they who were left had been given the land as their possession. But as is often the case, the Lord saw things in a way that people did not.

5. What did the Lord say about the exiles in **11:16–17?**

6. Read **11:18–21.** How would God work among these returnees? What would they do? What covenant promise did the Lord reaffirm (see **Genesis 17:7** and **Exodus 6:7**)?

7. What was to happen to those whose hearts were devoted to their idols **(11:21)?**

8. Read **11:22–23.** Recount the movement of the glory of the Lord. What did this mean?

9. Read **11:24–25.** Ezekiel was brought by the Spirit back to Babylonia where the vision ceased. Who were the recipients of Ezekiel's prophecy?

The Word for Us

1. According to **2 Peter 3:3–13** what do scoffers, like the leaders in Jerusalem, say about Jesus' coming to bring this world to an end? Why does He tarry? As we eagerly look forward to His coming, how should we live? To what do we have to look forward?

2. God promised to replace His people's stony heart with a heart of flesh. Read **Ephesians 3:14–4:3** and **Galatians 5:16–26.** How does the Holy Spirit work in our hearts? What is the result of that work?

Closing

Sing or read together the following stanzas of "Renew Me, O Eternal Light."

> Create in me a new heart, Lord,
> That gladly I obey Your Word.
> Let what You will be my desire,
> And with new life my soul inspire.
>
> Grant that I only You may love
> And seek those things which are above
> Till I behold You face to face,
> O Light eternal, through Your grace.

To Do This Week

Read **Ezekiel 33.** In addition you might want to read through **Ezekiel 12–32,** which will not be covered by this study.

Lesson 7

Ezekiel, Prophet of Restoration (Ezekiel 33)

Theme Verse

"So my mouth was opened and I was no longer silent" (**Ezekiel 33:22**).

Goal

We seek to understand the turning point in Ezekiel's ministry and in what ways his ministry after that point differed and in what ways it remained the same.

What's Going On Here?

The Word of God speaks both Law (the word of God that condemns) and Gospel (the Good News of salvation). The distinction is clearly seen in the book of **Ezekiel.** Interrupted by only an occasional word of hope, the content of the first 32 chapters of Ezekiel is unremitting judgment. It is the word of condemnation on sin repeated over and over again against the apostate people of Israel and against their neighbors who joined them in their idolatry. But beginning with **chapter 33** there is a change—and it is a dramatic change. Now the prophet who spoke only darkness and death, anger and destruction begins the tender words of restoration and renewal promised to the remnant referred to several times earlier in the book. As God once rescued the enslaved people from Egypt, so there would be a new exodus from Babylon and a return to the Promised Land.

The revived nation, however, was not to be an end in itself. The reestablished community would serve as a blueprint, a model, and a symbol of God's promise to restore all nations to fellowship with Him. This glorious future of the messianic kingdom is seen throughout the rest of the book. The new covenant is described in terms of the old political ordinances and ritual provisions. The immediate future and more distant scenes of prophecy merge to portray a grand panoramic view of worldwide redemption—Israel after the flesh returning to Jerusalem in the pledge that there would be an Israel of God consisting not only of Abraham's offspring but of all who have been "born again, not of perishable seed, but of imperishable, through the living and enduring word of God" (1 Peter 1:23).

Searching the Scriptures

In preparation for his new assignment as a prophet of restoration, the word of the Lord came to Ezekiel, renewing his commission as a watchman. Because the message of redemption was radically different than the threat of the wrath of God, Ezekiel might have concluded that it could be proclaimed on a different basis. Not so. The salvation to be offered was no group insurance. Only the repentant could avail themselves of it, and each person was responsible for his or her own response.

1. Read **Ezekiel 33:1–9.** What did the word of the Lord say about the prophet's responsibility? about the responsibility of individual hearers?

2. Read **33:10–11.** What was the attitude of the people when they finally faced their sin?

3. What was Ezekiel called to proclaim to these people? Note especially the oath with which the Lord began His declaration.

Read **33:12–20.** The people accused the Lord of being unjust in His dealings with them. But through Ezekiel, the Lord argued that it was not His ways that were unjust, but the ways of the people.

4. How would the Lord deal with a righteous person who trusted in the merits of his or her own righteousness, turned from righteous living, and began to do evil?

5. How would the Lord deal with the repentant person? How does the repentant person live?

6. Read **33:21–22.** These verses mark the turning point of Ezekiel's ministry and the reason for it. Recall that Ezekiel had been struck dumb by the Lord unless he had a message from the Lord to speak to the people. Read **3:26–27.** What word of judgment was in Ezekiel's inability to proclaim the word of the Lord?

7. Before Jerusalem fell, Ezekiel was told by the Lord that his mouth would be opened when he heard the news of its fall. Read **24:25–27** and **33:21–22.** What did the removal of Ezekiel's dumbness indicate?

8. Read **33:23–29.** Those people in Judah who had survived the destruction were trusting in the fact that they had escaped thus far. They reasoned that if the land had been given to Abraham, who was only one man, surely they who were more would inherit the land. Why were their hopes false (see **18:4–13** and **22:1–16**)? What was Ezekiel's message to them?

9. Read **33:30–33.** Ezekiel's next message was directed to his fellow exiles, who flocked to hear the messages from the Lord spoken by Ezekiel but who actually considered him more a source of entertainment than a prophet speaking the word of the Lord. What response to Ezekiel's message was lacking among these people **(33:31)?**

10. When would the people finally take Ezekiel seriously as a prophet of the Lord **(33:33)?**

The Word for Us

1. Compare the response of the people recorded in **Ezekiel 33:31** with Jesus' words in **Matthew 7:24–27.** What shows that a person takes the Word of the Lord seriously? What does that mean for a person's future? What things hinder you from doing that? From where does the power and motivation come to do it (see **2 Corinthians 1:21–22** and **Hebrews 13:20–21**)?

2. Compare **Ezekiel 33:11** with **Luke 15:1–7.** What is God's reaction when people repent? What was the reaction of the Pharisees and teachers of the law to Jesus' ministry to tax collectors and others considered by the religious leaders to be especially sinful? What motivates such reactions? What is your reaction when others repent? What can you remember that will help you share God's joy when others repent and receive His forgiveness?

Closing

Pray this prayer together:

Father in heaven, we thank You that You have led us to repentance and faith. Forgive us for the times when we have failed to put Your Word into practice and for the times when we have resented Your grace in the lives of others. Help us to share Your joy when others come to know Your love. Give us the wisdom and the ability to take Your Word seriously and put it into practice that our lives might glorify You and that at last we might come into the inheritance You have prepared for those who trust in Your mercy through Jesus Christ our Lord. Amen.

To Do This Week

Read **Ezekiel 34.**

Lesson 8

The Shepherd-King
(Ezekiel 34)

Theme Verse

"I will place over them one shepherd, My servant David, and He will tend them; He will tend them and be their shepherd" **(Ezekiel 34:23).**

Goal

We seek to understand the Lord's indictment of the shepherds of Israel and His promise to be their Shepherd and to place over them the Shepherd-King of David's line.

What's Going On Here?

Oriented in the principles governing the proclamation of the Gospel of restoration **(Ezekiel 33),** Ezekiel proceeded without delay to let the word of the Lord brighten the dismal world of sin and judgment with rays of redemptive grace. The light of revealed truth illumined not only the gloom of his day, but it shed its beams of salvation through future ages to the end of time. It brought into view the redeemed Israel of God, safe and happy, under the beneficent rule of the Lord's servant David, the messianic Prince (King). His subjects would not live in fear, for they would enjoy the blessings of renewed fellowship with their Creator, guaranteed by an everlasting covenant of peace.

As Ezekiel told of this restoration from judgment to bliss, we must remember that he saw it in the perspective of prophetic vision. Past, present, and future merged into a picture of timeless fact and unending duration. Events and circumstances in Israel's history became prophetic types of things to come and then appeared again with purely historical significance. The old covenant blended into the new.

And ancient Israel's restoration to safety and well-being served as a transparency through which can be seen outlined the features of God's kingdom, which Scripture describes also in the matter-of-fact language of fulfilled prophecy. Ezekiel told that after an apparent delay God's eternal plan to redeem humanity would get under way again. The chosen people, once abused by their own leaders and now scattered like lost sheep on the hills of foreign nations, would be brought back to the Promised Land. Out of their midst would arise a Prince of "the house and line of David" **(Luke 2:4).** Though not of this world, His kingdom would be worldwide. His subjects would constitute an international assembly, uniting those of every race and national affiliation. Under His reign they would be able to draw on God's inexhaustible resources. Even the poorest and the weakest would have access to all they needed for time and eternity. Finally, suffering in a heartless world and the injustice of every human social order would be left behind when the Shepherd-King would say: "Come, you who are blessed by My Father; take your inheritance, the kingdom prepared for you since the creation of the world" **(Matthew 25:34).**

Searching the Scriptures

1. Read **34:1–10.** What did Israel's political and religious leaders do to fleece the flock according to **verses 2–3?**

2. What did they fail to do according to **verse 4?** What did they do instead?

3. What was the result according to **verses 5–6?**

4. In what way was the situation still the same at Jesus' time according to **Matthew 9:36?**

5. God called the Israelites "My sheep" **(v. 6).** Why were they of special concern to Him according to **Exodus 19:4–6?** See also **Psalm 95:7; 100:3.**

6. God likewise called Israel's leaders "My shepherds" **(v. 8)** because they were to be His representatives. What action in the consecration of a king **(1 Samuel 16:11–13; 1 Kings 1:34),** a prophet **(1 Kings 19:16),** and a priest **(Exodus 28:41)** expressed this relationship? What did the action indicate about the task?

But the shepherds of Israel did not fulfill their calling. Therefore, the Lord declared that He would hold them accountable for the flock, remove them from tending the flock, and rescue the flock from their hands **(v. 10).**

7. Read **34:11–16.** What would the Lord Himself do for His flock?

8. Read **34:17–24.** The people of ancient Israel did not suffer only from evil shepherds, but in the flock itself there were fat sheep (fat cats) and rams and goats who preyed on the weak and lean sheep. How malicious

were they in seeking their advantage according to **verses 18–19?**

Such actions indicate that human society cannot pull itself up from the quicksands of corruption by its own bootstraps. If the power and reign of sin was to be broken, God had to establish the kingdom of His servant David.

9. What would great David's greater Son do for the sheep according to **John 10:14–16?** How long will the Shepherd-Prince rule according to **Ezekiel 37:25?** Note how His human ancestry from royal David's house is asserted in **2 Samuel 7:11–16; Isaiah 9:6–7; 11:1–5;** and **Jeremiah 23:5–6.** In contrast to the evil shepherds, what will characterize the rule of this Shepherd?

10. Read **34:25–31.** The perfect bliss to be enjoyed by the Shepherd's subjects when He is Prince among them is described in terms of earthly prosperity and security. This state of well-being will prevail because, in the reign of this servant David, God will establish a covenant of peace with sin-cursed humanity. (*Shalom*, the Hebrew word for "peace" denotes not only the absence of conflict, but harmony, wholeness, and well-being.) As if signing His name to a contract, God promised to bring His rebellious creatures into the perfect relationship with Him that existed in the Garden of Eden. For the bliss of restored fellowship with God described as paradise regained, see **Amos 9:13; Isaiah 11:6–9; 35:5–10; Revelation 22:1–5.** What hope do these passages bring? What do they mean to your faith in Jesus as Savior? What does the Prince of peace provide to make possible restored peace with God according to **Colossians 1:13–20?**

The Word for Us

1. Jesus, the Good Shepherd, says that His sheep constitute one flock (**John 10:16**). What is it that makes them one flock (see **John 17:20–21; Ephesians 4:3–6**)? How did we become members of the flock? What assurance does the Good Shepherd give us in **John 10:27–30** that we will always remain in His protection?

2. Part of the way the Good Shepherd cares for His flock is through the gift of pastors. Read **1 Peter 5:1–2.** What responsibility do pastors carry? According to **Hebrews 13:7, 17–18** and **Ephesians 6:19–20,** what can you do to support your pastor in his ministry? What other things can you think of?

Closing

Sing or read together this rendering of **Psalm 23,** "The Lord's My Shepherd, I'll Not Want."

> The Lord's my shepherd, I'll not want;
> He makes me down to lie
> In pastures green; He leadeth me
> The quiet waters by.
>
> My soul He doth restore again
> And me to walk doth make
> Within the paths of righteousness,
> E'en for His own name's sake.
>
> Yea, though I walk in death's dark vale,
> Yet will I fear no ill;
> For Thou art with me, and Thy rod
> And staff me comfort still.
>
> My table Thou has furnished
> In presence of my foes;
> My head Thou dost with oil anoint,
> And my cup overflows.
>
> Goodness and mercy all my life
> Shall surely follow me;
> And in God's house forevermore
> My dwelling place shall be.

To Do This Week

Read **Ezekiel 37.** You might also want to read **Ezekiel 35–36,** which will not be covered by this study.

Lesson 9

Restoration to Life (Ezekiel 37)

Theme Verse

"This is what the Sovereign LORD says: O my people, I am going to open your graves and bring you up from them; I will bring you back to the land of Israel" (**Ezekiel 37:12**).

Goal

We seek to understand Ezekiel's vision of the dry bones, its message, and Ezekiel's description of the messianic kingdom. In addition we will look at general characteristics of prophecy and how to interpret it correctly.

What's Going On Here?

In **Ezekiel 34** God promised to do marvelous things to carry out His plan to redeem humanity, seemingly halted by the capture of Jerusalem and the dispersion of the chosen people. The word of the Lord recorded in **Ezekiel 35** brought the solemn assurance that nothing would be able to prevent the coming reign of the Good Shepherd. Hostile forces, represented by Israel's inveterate foe Edom, would go down to defeat because they had attempted to take advantage of Israel's defeat and claim the Promised Land. The destruction of Jerusalem and the humiliating exile of its inhabitants were not evidence of the God of Israel's inability to ward off the disaster, as the heathen claimed. On the contrary, the heathen invaders acted only by God's permission and only followed His bidding when He needed them as His rod of anger on a land defiled by idol worship. Therefore, when the proper time had come and He had cleansed the penitent Israelites, He would be able also to order the conqueror to set the captives free (**36:16–37**).

Ezekiel's hearers still did not greet these glad tidings with cheers and jubilation. Their response was a doleful lament of despair: "Our bones are dried up and our hope is gone; we are cut off" **(37:11).** However, the Shepherd sought His sheep even when they strayed into the desolate land of hopelessness and doubt. Ezekiel was called to persuade the doubters that they had no reason to despair if they believed in a Creator who calls into existence that which previously did not exist **(Romans 4:17; Deuteronomy 32:39; Psalm 33:8–9).**

Searching the Scriptures

1. Read **Ezekiel 37:1–3.** The Spirit of the Lord transported Ezekiel in a vision to a valley. What did Ezekiel see on the valley floor? What did the Lord ask Ezekiel, and how did he respond? Did the Lord's suggestion seem likely?

2. Read **37:4–10.** What enabled the dry bones to come to life? This was a two-stage process. What other creation was accomplished in a similar two-staged manner (see **Genesis 2:7**)?

The things represented by the English words *spirit, breath,* and *wind* are represented in Hebrew by one word, *ruakh* (the *kh* is pronounced with a guttural *k* sound). That word is used throughout this section of **Ezekiel 37.** While English translators had to pick one English word to translate *ruakh* in each instance, each occurrence also carries nuances of the other meanings.

At its root *ruah* denotes the sense of 'air in motion', *i.e.* wind or breath. ... It comes to mean both man's spirit, or disposition, and also emotional qualities like vigour, courage, impatience and ecstasy. It covers not only man's vital breath, given to him at birth and leaving his body in his dying gasp, but also the Spirit of God who imparts that breath (John B. Taylor, *Ezekiel: An Introduction and Commentary* [Downers Grove, IL: Inter-Varsity Press, 1969], p. 237).

To get a feel for the use of this word in Hebrew, reread **37:1–10,** substituting *ruakh* each time you see *spirit, breath,* or *wind.*

3. The number of people that Ezekiel saw after they came back to life was not small. How were the people described in **37:10?**

4. Read **37:11–14.** What did the dry bones represent? What did their coming to life represent? Who alone could accomplish this?

5. What would the people know when the Lord had accomplished what He promised **(37:13–14)?** What special gift would the Lord give to His people as they returned to their land?

The return of God's people to their land was the next step in God's plan to save humanity from sin, death, and Satan and bring them into fellowship with Himself through His Messiah. Through Ezekiel as through other prophets, God foretold the coming of that Messiah and revealed aspects of the kingdom the Messiah would establish. Because much of the rest of **Ezekiel** looks forward to the messianic age, it will be helpful before we proceed to examine some characteristics of biblical prophecy and principles for correctly interpreting it. You might want to consult the book *Prophecy Interpreted* by John P. Milton for a more complete discussion of this topic (Minneapolis: Augsburg, 1960).

One characteristic of prophecy is a shortened time perspective. The prophets sometimes saw events in the near future and the distant future in the same picture. Rarely were they concerned with establishing a chronology of coming events. "In the prophetic message the eschatological [end-times] goal of the covenant is often seen as coming soon. It seems to be expected right after and in direct relation to the historical situation of the moment to which the message of the prophet is directed" (Milton, p. 15).

The prophets often described the future messianic kingdom in terms related to their time and their culture. This " 'times-coloring' does not belong to the essence of a prophecy: it is rather the historical form in which the abiding truth of the prophecy is temporarily clothed. A prophecy may be much more spiritual and far more universal than a literal interpretation of this 'times-coloring' would indicate" (Milton, p. 11).

The key to interpreting such passages is "to distinguish between that which is the very essence of a promise, or its central idea, and that which belongs to the temporary forms of which God made use in bringing the promise to fulfillment. We must learn to distinguish, too, between the eternal and the transient in prophecy" (Milton, p. 71).

Finally, we will want to remember that the fulfillment of a prophecy is often greater than the prediction, that is, that the fulfillment

> is clearer, that it is more specific in reference, that it has a more definite spiritual emphasis. The old covenant becomes the new. The kingly reign of Yahve [Yahweh] over His people Israel becomes the universal and eternal reign of the King of kings and the Lord of lords. Israel as the people of God becomes the Church of Jesus Christ. ... There *is* predictive prophecy in the Old Testament; but we need the commentary of redemptive history, or of the New Testament gospel, *to declare all that was really essential in the prophecy* (Milton, pp. 20–21).

Keeping these ideas in mind, let's return to **Ezekiel 37**. Read **37:15–28.**

In this section, Ezekiel blended aspects of the messianic kingdom with the return of the Israelites to their own land. Using imagery of an ideal life in that land, he described the messianic age.

6. What was the central idea behind Ezekiel's symbolic action and its explanation **(37:15–23)?**

7. How did Ezekiel describe the messianic age (**37:23–28**)?

8. What in Ezekiel's description belonged to his time and not to the essence of the prophecy (**37:25**)?

9. Read **Luke 1:26–35; Matthew 26:26–29; John 18:36; Matthew 24:30–31; Revelation 5:9–10; 21:1–4, 22.** Has Ezekiel's prophecy been fulfilled? How is (will be) the fulfillment greater than the prediction?

The Word for Us

1. The Greek word *pneuma*, like the Hebrew word *ruakh*, can mean "breathe," "wind," or "spirit." How did Jesus describe the work of the Holy Spirit in **John 3:8?** How has the Holy Spirit worked in your life? See **John 3:1–8** and the Third Article of the Apostles' Creed and Martin Luther's explanation of it as follows:

> I believe in the Holy Spirit, the holy Christian church, the communion of saints, the forgiveness of sins, the resurrection of the body, and the life everlasting. Amen.

What does this mean? I believe that I cannot by my own reason or strength believe in Jesus Christ, my Lord, or come to Him; but the Holy Spirit has called me by the Gospel, enlightened me with His gifts, sanctified and kept me in the true faith.

In the same way He calls, gathers, enlightens, and sanctifies the whole Christian church on earth, and keeps it with Jesus Christ in the one true faith.

In this Christian church He daily and richly forgives all my sins and the sins of all believers.

On the Last Day He will raise me and all the dead, and give eternal life to me and all believers in Christ.

This is most certainly true. (from the Small Catechism)

2. Although Ezekiel's vision of the dry bones is an analogy and does not deal with actual resurrection from the dead, it does affirm that God rules even over death. What additional affirmation of that truth did the Old Testament people have in **1 Kings 17:17–24** and **2 Kings 4:8–37?** Compare **Job 19:25–27; Psalm 49:15; 73:24; Isaiah 26:19; Daniel 12:2.** Using these Scripture texts, what conclusions about God's power over death can you determine? How do those truths apply to Jesus? What do they mean for us?

Closing

Sing or read together the following stanzas of "To God the Holy Spirit Let Us Pray":

To God the Holy Spirit let us pray
Most of all for faith upon our way
That He may defend us when life is ending
And from exile home we are wending.
Lord, have mercy!

Shine in our hearts, O Spirit, precious light;
Teach us Jesus Christ to know aright
That we may abide in the Lord who bought us,
Till to our true home He has brought us.
Lord, have mercy!

To Do This Week

Read **Ezekiel 38–39.**

Lesson 10

Restoration to Safety
(Ezekiel 38–39)

Theme Verse

"Son of man, set your face against Gog, of the land of Magog, the chief prince of Meshech and Tubal; prophesy against him" **(Ezekiel 38:2)**.

Goal

We seek to understand Ezekiel's prophecy about the final assault of the forces of evil against God and His people and how the Lord Himself will fight for His people in that battle and win a complete and final victory.

What's Going On Here?

The promise of unalloyed bliss, held out in the preceding chapter, suggests this question: Will the servant David, the one King of one nation, actually establish an everlasting covenant and rule forever, or will sinister forces combine to destroy His reign of peace? **Chapters 38–39** give the answer: Yes, there will be vicious and formidable enemies, but their attacks will fail and end in their own destruction. In giving this assurance of safety, Ezekiel's prophetic vision peers through future ages down to the end of time.

Searching the Scriptures

Review the characteristics of biblical prophecy and the principles for correctly interpreting it following question 5 in the previous lesson.

In addition, it is necessary when looking at these two chapters of **Ezekiel** to recognize that they contain apocalyptic language. Apocalyptic is a type of literature of which the book of **Revelation** is the clearest example in the Bible. But some characteristics of apocalyptic literature are found here in **Ezekiel 38–39.** A prominent feature of apocalyptic literature found in these chapters is symbolic language. Another is a focus on the end of history.

In his commentary on **Ezekiel,** John B. Taylor provides a word of caution about interpreting these chapters:

> The language is the language of apocalyptic: it is largely symbolical and at times deliberately shadowy and even cryptic. But though the details are vague, the main thrust is clearly and boldly expressed. Interpretation therefore needs to correspond to contents, and attempts to read too much into the incidentals of the prophecy betray the ingenuity of the speculator rather than the sobriety of the exegete (*Ezekiel: An Introduction and Commentary* [Downers Grove, IL: Inter-Varsity Press, 1969], p. 243).

In addition to the Lord, the main characters in the drama played out in these chapters are Israel and the leader Gog and his forces. Israel, rescued from the Babylonian exile and allowed to dwell securely in its promised homeland **(38:11),** serves as the symbol and type of the one holy Christian church, restored to life and communion with God and blessed with peace by the Good Shepherd who gave His life for His flock. Gog and his hordes represent enemies of God and His people, most likely including both earthly and demonic forces of evil.

Ezekiel 38:16 tells us that the advance of Gog and his forces against the people of God would happen "in days to come." The Hebrew phrase here translated "in days to come" is often translated "in the last days." This phrase was used by the prophets to denote various periods of the messianic era—that era that began with the coming of the Messiah and will extend forever into eternity (see for example **Isaiah 2:2–4**). Here in **Ezekiel,** the focus seems to be on the period immediately preceding Judgment Day. At that time God's enemies would make a supreme effort to destroy His kingdom. But they would not succeed. Using images and place names from his time in history, Ezekiel several times in these two chapters pictured the final defeat of the forces of evil arrayed against the Lord and His church.

Read **Ezekiel 38:1–6.** Various attempts have been made to identify Gog with an ancient ruler who would have been a prototype of this leader of God's enemies. However, an exact identification is not certain. In **Genesis 10:2,** Magog, Meshech, Tubal, and Gomer are all listed as sons of Japheth (one of Noah's sons). In **Genesis 10:3,** Togarmah is listed as a son of Gomer. The descendants of these men and thus the peoples referred to in **Ezekiel** lived in Asia Minor and around the Black Sea (see the note on **Genesis 10:2** in the Concordia Self-Study Bible and the accompanying map on page 20). Thus as in the past (with Assyria and Babylon), the enemy of God's people was pictured as coming from the north. The forces from the north would be joined by forces from the east (Persia) and from the south (Cush and Put were in Africa).

1. Even before knowing what Gog's intentions were, what was Ezekiel instructed to prophesy against Gog? What does this tell us about the certainty of Gog's defeat?

2. Read **38:7–16.** How are God's people described in **verses 8** and **11?** What might be the reason for their defenselessness?

3. What would be Gog's evil scheme **(38:11–12)?** What would be the attitude of other nations **(38:13)?**

4. According to **38:8,** when would these events take place? How vast would be the forces at Gog's command **(38:9)?**

5. Compare **38:10** and **38:16.** Who would be behind Gog's scheme? What would be the Lord's purpose?

Read **38:17–23.** Gog is not mentioned by name anywhere else in Scripture except **Revelation;** the reference to earlier prophecies in **verse 17** is likely a general reference to prophecies of God's judgment on the nations hostile to Him and His people.

6. What would happen at Gog's invasion **(38:18)?**

7. Who would fight for defenseless Israel? What would be the weapons used by this defender? Against whom would Gog's army end up fighting?

Ezekiel's description of this battle parallels the descriptions of other prophets of the day of the Lord, the culmination of God's wrath against His enemies and the final deliverance of God's people, the ending of this world and the ushering in of the new heavens and the new earth. As you have time, read some of these other passages: **Joel 2:28–32; Zephaniah 1:14–18; Isaiah 66:12–24; Zechariah 12:1–10; 14:1–16.**

Reread **Ezekiel 38:23.** Note again that through the defeat of His enemies, God would show His greatness and His holiness and reveal Himself to the nations as the Lord of the earth.

Many authors of the Old Testament delighted in using repetition. Ezekiel was no exception. In **Ezekiel 39,** we again read of the defeat of Gog.

As you read, notice the use of the number *seven.* When used in a symbolic way in Scripture, the number *seven* represents completeness and totality; it was a favorite of apocalyptic writers.

8. Read **39:1–16.** What assurance is given in **verses 5** and **8** that all this would come to pass?

9. How is the completeness and finality of the enemy's defeat pictured?

Read **39:17–20.** In these verses, Ezekiel reverted back to **verse 4** and described in detail how, at God's invitation, the animals and birds would gorge themselves on the flesh of God's enemies. The imagery of a sacrifice suggests that the dead bodies would be devoted to the Lord as happened with all that was taken in the conquest of Jericho (see **Joshua 6:17**).

10. What does such a graphic description communicate about God's judgment? Why is that important?

Read **39:21–29.** Note the shortened time perspective. The events pictured earlier in the chapter and referred to in **verse 21,** though they would not take place for centuries, are related to the exile.

11. Because of the exile, the Lord's holy name was profaned both in Israel, whose people thought that God had abandoned them, and in other nations, whose people said that God was unable to protect His people. When the Lord has displayed His glory among the nations by inflicting punishment on them, what would Israel know about the Lord (**39:22**)? What would the nations know (**39:23–24**)?

12. What two things would the Lord do as He brought His people back to their land and settled them in safety (**39:25**)?

13. What do the promises of **39:29** mean for God's people?

The Word for Us

1. Sometimes circumstances in our lives and in the world in general tempt us to think that God is not in control or that He no longer cares for us. How might these chapters of **Ezekiel** encourage us at such times?

2. In recent years it has been popular in some Christian circles to identify places such as Meshech and Tubal with modern places and to try to map out in detail how prophecies such as those in **Ezekiel 38–39** might be fulfilled in our day. Such theories are usually based on faulty biblical interpretation and amount to little more than speculation. They have the danger of distracting people from the central message of the Gospel—forgiveness of sins through Christ—and the central mission of the church—proclaiming repentance and forgiveness in Jesus' name to all people. Read **Matthew 24:36–51** and **Acts 1:6–8.** What did Jesus say about our ability to know when He would return and the end of the world would come? What is to be our attitude and what are we to be doing while we await that day?

Closing

Sing or read together the following stanzas of "Do Not Despair, O Little Flock."

Do not despair, O little flock,
Although the foes' fierce battle shock
Loud on all sides assail you!
Though at your fall they laugh, secure,
Their triumph cannot long endure;
Let not your courage fail you!

The cause is God's; obey His call
And to His hand commit your all
And fear no ill impending!
Though not yet seen by human eyes,
His Gideon shall for you arise,
God's Word and you defending.

As sure as God's own Word is true,
Not Satan, hell, nor all their crew
Can stand against His power.
Scorn and contempt their cup will fill,
For God is with His people still,
Their help and their strong tower.

Then help us, Lord! Now hear our prayer.
Defend Your people ev'rywhere
For Your own name's sake. Amen.
Then with a mighty hymn of praise
Your Church in earth and heav'n will raise
Their songs of triumph. Amen.

To Do This Week

Skim **Ezekiel 40–48.** Selected portions will be studied in the next lesson.

Lesson 11

"The Lord Is There" (Ezekiel 40–48)

Theme Verse

"The name of the city from that time on will be: THE LORD IS THERE" (**Ezekiel 48:35**).

Goal

We seek to understand Ezekiel's vision of the Lord returning to dwell among His people and what it meant for them and what it means for us.

What's Going On Here?

The last nine chapters of **Ezekiel (40–48)** record what the prophet saw and heard when, in visions of God, he was transported from Babylon to a very high mountain in the land of Israel. In the vision, Ezekiel was shown, in images from his time, in images of the old covenant, aspects of the messianic age. The key theme throughout the vision was the Lord again dwelling in the midst of His people. In this lesson, we will look at selected portions of that vision.

Searching the Scriptures

1. Read **Ezekiel 40:1–4.** A heavenly being, a man who had the appearance of bronze, was to escort Ezekiel throughout the vision. What special instructions did he give Ezekiel at the outset?

Recall that in the old covenant, the temple was the place where the Lord graciously localized His presence among His people. In his vision, Ezekiel was first given a tour of an ideal temple complex. He was made aware that the kind of temple the Lord honors with His presence is not a matter of indifference. Beginning at **40:5** and continuing through **chapter 41,** Ezekiel recorded the features of the temple as he saw them in minute detail and at great length. Yet as specific as the dimensions and measurements are, they are not complete enough to be an architect's blueprint. Lacking are such important items as the height of the various structures and the kind of material to be used in the construction. But for this structure, a builder's drawing and instructions were not necessary. Ezekiel's heavenly guide led him through a structure that was already built and was ready for inspection and use.

Those who are interested might at a later time read through **Ezekiel 40:5–42:20,** following a diagram such as the one on page 1287 of the Concordia Self-Study Bible.

2. From among the jumble of specifications, one overall, distinctive feature emerges. Read **41:13–14; 42:15–20.** What is that feature? What do you think that feature symbolizes?

3. Read **43:1–12.** Here Ezekiel saw the reversal of what he had seen earlier when the glory of the Lord had departed from the temple in Jerusalem and had stopped above the mountain east of the city **(9:3; 10:5–8, 18–19; 11:22–23).** What did Ezekiel's vision of the return of the Lord's glory to the temple mean?

4. At the beginning of Ezekiel's ministry, the voice of the Lord commanded Ezekiel to speak the Lord's words to His people **(2:7).** Until the city fell, those words were mostly words of judgment. In this vision,

Ezekiel heard the voice of the Lord again. What did the Lord promise in **43:7**?

5. In case the people had not yet understood the message, the Lord emphasized again that He would not share the worship of His people with idols. What was Ezekiel's description of the temple meant to invoke in its hearers **(43:10–11)**? What action were the people to take so that the Lord could dwell with them **(43:9)**?

Ezekiel's prophecy of a temple where God would dwell forever with His people was fulfilled in a limited way when the exiles returned to Israel and rebuilt the temple. But it had a larger fulfillment. It pointed forward to the new covenant, in which all humanity was restored to communion with God "through the sacrifice of the body of Jesus Christ once for all" **(Hebrews 10:10)** on the cross of Calvary. As a result, all who receive His atoning sacrifice for their sins are counted worthy to be built into "a holy temple in the Lord," "a dwelling in which God lives by His Spirit" **(Ephesians 2:19–22)**. "Like living stones," they are "built into a spiritual house to be a holy priesthood, offering spiritual sacrifices acceptable to God through Jesus Christ" **(1 Peter 2:5)**, offering their "bodies as living sacrifices, holy and pleasing to God" **(Romans 12:1)**.

6. Ezekiel's prophecy will have yet a greater and a final fulfillment. Read **Revelation 21:1–4, 22.** When and where will Ezekiel's prophecy be completely fulfilled?

The next part of Ezekiel's vision (43:13–46:24) dealt mostly with themes related to the central issue of worship, of how people may draw near to God and celebrate their restored communion with Him. The worship by which they would be permitted to come into His presence was patterned after the rituals prescribed by the old covenant and enacted in Solomon's temple.

But, while the structure and furnishings of Ezekiel's temple and the worship within its walls had much in common with the building erected by Solomon and the ritual prescribed for it in the law of Moses, there were significant differences. Although there was mention of different types of offerings and the atonement they made for the people (45:15–17), conspicuously absent were some other rites symbolizing the worshipers' need of atonement, of purification and forgiveness, as they came into the presence of God. There was no mention of the ark of the covenant. Previously, blood sprinkled on its lid, called the atonement cover (or mercy seat), signified that a sacrifice was required in order to approach God. In Ezekiel's vision, there was no longer a need for the office of high priest—the one who alone could enter the Most Holy Place of the temple to bring the reconciling offering. Finally, there was no mention of the Day of Atonement, that great annual festival when the ritual of atonement took place.

7. Read **Hebrews 7:26–28; 9:11–14.** What do we now recognize as the reason why these acts and rituals are no longer necessary?

8. Read **Ezekiel 47:1–12.** Describe the source of this river and its unique properties. What does this river symbolize?

Read **Genesis 2:8–14.** The antecedent for this imagery in Ezekiel's vision is probably the tree of life and the river that watered the Garden of Eden. In his vision, Ezekiel saw the restoration of the blessings lost to humanity because of their sin. Those who have faith in Christ have been brought from spiritual death to life by Him who gives them to drink of life-giving water (see **John 4:10–14; 7:37–39**). But our full enjoyment of the water of life is yet to come.

9. Read **Revelation 22:1–5.** When will we enjoy the blessings of the water of life fully? Why will that be possible?

In the last part of his vision (recorded in **Ezekiel 48**), Ezekiel saw the division of the land of Israel into portions for each of the 12 tribes. Then he saw the 12 gates of the city of Jerusalem, each named after one of the tribes. (These gates were also seen by John in his vision of the new Jerusalem **[Revelation 21:12–14]**). In a grand finale, Ezekiel was shown the name of the city from that time on: "THE LORD IS THERE" **(48:35).**

10. Why is this a fitting ending to Ezekiel's vision and his book? Compare **Revelation 21:1–4.**

The Word for Us

1. According to the date given in **Ezekiel 40:1,** Ezekiel's vision recorded at the end of his book took place 13 years after the destruction of Jerusalem. During all that time, Ezekiel had been proclaiming that the exiles would return home, but nothing had happened to make his promise of restoration come true. The temple was still in ruins and the people still in exile. What promise does God make in **Isaiah 55:10–11?** During times

of trouble in our lives, we often strain under the seeming slowness of God to hear and answer our prayers. During those times, what insights from Scripture can help us? How can we encourage one another? Much of Ezekiel's vision of the future was not complete in his lifetime and will not come to fulfillment until the end of time. What does that fact tell us about God and our expectations of Him? Why can we be certain God will act according to His promises?

2. As we have seen, much of **Ezekiel** deals with the temple, the place where God resided among His people in the Old Testament. We have also looked at **Revelation 21,** which proclaims that in heaven no temple will be needed because God Himself will dwell directly with His people. But what about the period between those times, the period in which we live now? Read **1 Corinthians 3:1–17.** What does Paul say here about Christ's church? What does that mean about how we should treat the church? Read **1 Corinthians 6:18–20.** Why can Paul say that our bodies are the temple of the Holy Spirit? What does that mean for how we treat our bodies? What are we to do with them?

Closing

Read responsively the following words from **Revelation (22:12–14, 20–21):**

Leader: [Jesus said,] "Behold, I am coming soon! ... I am the Alpha and the Omega, the First and the Last, the Beginning and the End. Blessed are those who wash their robes, that they may have the right to the tree of life and may go through the gates into the city." ... "Yes, I am coming soon."

Participants: Amen. Come, Lord Jesus.

Leader: The grace of the Lord Jesus be with God's people. Amen.

EZEKIEL

I Am the LORD

Leaders Notes

Preparing to Teach Ezekiel

In preparation to teach, consult the introduction to the book of Ezekiel in the Concordia Self-Study Bible, and if possible, read the section on Ezekiel in the *Concordia Self-Study Commentary* (CPH, 1979).

Also read the text in a modern translation. The NIV is referred to in the lesson comments.

In the section "Searching the Scriptures," the leader guides discussion, using the questions given (or others) to help the class discover what the text actually says. This is a major part of teaching, namely, directing the learners to discover for themselves.

Another major portion of each lesson is "The Word for Us." This section helps participants, through discussion, to see the meaning of the text for our times, for our church and world today, and especially for our own lives.

Group Bible Study

Group Bible study means mutual learning from one another under the guidance of a leader or facilitator. The Bible is an inexhaustible resource. No one person can discover all it has to offer. In a class many eyes see many things and can apply them to many life situations. The leader should resist the temptation to "give the answers" and so act as an "authority." This teaching approach stifles participation by individual members and can actually hamper learning. As a general rule the teacher is not to "give interpretation" but to "develop interpreters." Of course there are times when the leader should and must share insights and information gained by his or her own deeper research. The ideal class is one in which the leader guides class members through the lesson and engages them in meaningful sharing and discussion at all points, leading them to a summary of the lesson at the close. As a general rule, don't explain what the learners can discover by themselves.

Have a chalkboard and chalk or newsprint and marker available to emphasize significant points of the lesson. Put your inquiries or the inquiries of participants into questions, problems, or issues. This provokes thought. Keep discussion to the point. List on a chalkboard, marker board, or newsprint the answers given. Then determine the most vital points made in the discussion. Ask additional questions to fill apparent gaps.

The aim of every Bible study is to help people grow spiritually, not merely in biblical and theological knowledge, but in Christian thinking and living. This means growth in Christian attitudes, insights, and skills for Christian living. The focus of this course must be the church and the world of our day. The guiding question will be this: What does the Lord teach us for life today through the book of Ezekiel?

Pace Your Teaching

Depending on the time you have, you may not want to cover every question in each lesson. This may lead to undue haste and frustration. Be selective. Pace your teaching. Spend no more than five to 10 minutes with "Theme Verse," "Goal," and "What's Going On Here?" Take time to go into the text by topic, but not word by word. Get the sweep of meaning. Occasionally stop to help the class gain understanding of a word or concept. Allow approximately 10 to 15 minutes for "The Word for Us." Allowing approximately five minutes for "Closing" and announcements, you will notice, allows you only approximately 30 minutes for "Searching the Scriptures."

Should your group have more than a one-hour class period, you can take it more leisurely. But do not allow any lesson to drag and become tiresome. Keep it moving. Keep it alive. Keep it meaningful. Eliminate some questions and restrict yourself to those questions most meaningful to the members of the class. If most members study the text at home, they can report their findings, and the time gained can be applied to relating the lesson to life.

Good Preparation

Good preparation by the leader usually affects the satisfaction the class will experience.

Suggestions to the Leader for Using the Study Guide

The Lesson Pattern

This set of 11 lessons is based on a significant and timely Old Testament book—Ezekiel. The material is designed to aid *Bible study*, that is, to aid a consideration of the written Word of God, with discussion and personal application growing out of the text at hand.

The typical lesson is divided into these sections:
1. Theme Verse
2. Goal
3. What's Going On Here?
4. Searching the Scriptures
5. The Word for Us
6. Closing
7. To Do This Week

"Theme Verse," "Goal," and "What's Going On Here?" give the leader assistance in arousing the interest of the group in the concepts of the chapter. Here the leader stimulates minds. Do not linger too long over the introductory remarks.

"Searching the Scriptures" provides the real spade work necessary for Bible study. Here the class digs, uncovers, and discovers; it gets the facts and observes them. Comment from the leader is needed only to the extent that it helps the group understand the text. The same is true of looking up the indicated parallel passages. The questions in the study guide, arranged under subheadings and corresponding to sections within the text, are intended to help the participants discover the meaning of the text.

Having determined what the text says, the class is ready to apply the message. Having heard, read, marked, and learned the Word of God, proceed to digest it inwardly through discussion, evaluation, and application. This is done, as the study guide suggests, by taking the truths found in Ezekiel and applying them to the world and Christianity, in general, and then to personal Christian life. Class time may not permit discussion of all questions and topics. In preparation the leader may need to select one or two and focus on them. These questions bring God's message to the individual Christian. Close the session by reviewing one important truth from the lesson.

Remember, the Word of God is sacred, but the study guide is not. The guide offers only suggestions. The leader should not hesitate to alter the guidelines or substitute others to meet his or her needs and the needs of the participants. Adapt your teaching plan to your class and your class period. Good teaching directs the learner to discover for himself or herself. For the teacher this means directing the learner, not giving the learner answers. Choose the verses that should be looked up in Scripture. What discussion questions will you ask? At what points? Write them in the margin of your study guide. Involve class members, but give them clear directions. What practical actions might you propose for the week following the lesson? A trip to the slums? Interviewing a poor family? Talking about injustice with a county or city administrator? Which of the items do you consider most important for your class?

How will you best use your teaching period? Do you have 45 minutes? an hour? or an hour and a half? If time is short, what should you cut? Learn to become a wise steward of class time.

Be sure to take time to summarize the lesson, or have a class member do it. Plan brief opening and closing devotions using members of the class. In addition, remember to pray frequently for yourself and your class.

Lesson 1

The Glory of the Lord

Theme Verse

Invite a volunteer to read aloud the theme verse.

Goal

Read aloud the goal statement for this lesson.

What's Going On Here?

This section provides a context for studying **Ezekiel.** Invite volunteers to read this section paragraph-by-paragraph. Then read aloud **Ezekiel 1.**

Searching the Scriptures

1. The north was the place from which the Lord sent destruction upon Judah. That destruction had been foretold by Jeremiah; therefore, the people of God knew that it was God who controlled the north.

2. Both **Ezekiel** and **Nahum** reveal that God uses the stormy wind as a vehicle of His coming. The storm is a manifestation of God's might.

3. In **Deut. 4:24** and **Is. 10:17,** the Lord is likened to a fire, a fire that will consume His enemies and bring His judgment. Jerusalem will indeed be burned by the Babylonians as a judgment on God's people, but that will happen at God's direction.

4. Prophets of the Lord had seen God sitting on His throne. Knowing that God was sitting on the kingly throne of the universe could have enabled the exiles to remember that God is in control despite the circumstances.

5. The chariot that Ezekiel saw might have brought to mind the heavenly chariot that came to take Elijah to heaven. Habakkuk poetically recalled the Lord riding to victory in His chariots. Again the exiles could have found comfort in the fact that the Lord, not Marduk, was the rider of victory chariots.

6. One cherub was on each end of the atonement cover, which was the lid of the ark of the covenant. The ark of the covenant was placed in the Most Holy Place, first in the tabernacle and then later in the temple. In the space between the cherubim, the Lord's presence was localized in a special way among His people. Thus the atonement cover became known as the Lord's throne, and He was described as the one enthroned between the cherubim.

7. Nothing escapes the notice of a creature or vehicle full of eyes. This ability comes from the all-seeing God and is used in His service.

8. God dwells in unapproachable light and cannot be seen face to face by people lest they die.

9. The usual dwelling place of the Lord's glory was first the tabernacle and later the temple. Although God in His grace had localized His presence among His people in a special place, He was not bound to that place. The Lord's glory appearing to Ezekiel showed that the Lord was among His people in exile. In this they could take great comfort.

10. The Israelites could have remembered how after the flood the Lord had graciously promised never again to destroy the earth with a flood and had given the rainbow as a sign of that covenant. They could have looked forward to God's merciful favor beyond the darkness of the present judgment.

The Word for Us

1. Jesus, both God and man, is the only person who has ever seen the Father directly. God is the source of our life and the one with whom we were created to have fellowship, but we were alienated from God by our sin. Jesus has made God known to us and has opened the way to fellowship with Him for us. It is only through Jesus that we have access to the Father.

2. God's revelation to Ezekiel came from outside Ezekiel. It was not sought by Ezekiel, and he did nothing to bring it about. Ezekiel was given a peek of the heavenly realm, which is usually hidden from people during their earthly lives, but his consciousness did not merge with God. In fact in the vision, God revealed Himself as totally distinct from, yet involved with, His creation.

3. Both John and Ezekiel heard a voice and saw a vision of God on His throne. The throne in both cases was on a crystal clear expanse and was encircled by a rainbow. Their descriptions of the one on the throne differ but have in common the idea of majesty and brilliance. Both visions included elements of a storm. Both John and Ezekiel saw living creatures. In Ezekiel these creatures propelled the chariot under the throne. In John's vision, they were praising God. In Ezekiel each had two wings and four faces: one of a man, one of a lion, one of an ox, and one of an eagle. John saw that each creature had six wings and each had a different form and face. One was like a lion, one was like an ox, one had the face of a man, and one was like a flying eagle. In John's vision the creatures were covered with eyes, but in Ezekiel the eyes were on the wheels of the chariot. John's vision included 24 elders and seven lamps which were absent from Ezekiel's vision. It seems that John was looking directly into heaven, while the throne of God traveled to Ezekiel. Both visions contain the comforting

and faith-strengthening message that despite what is happening to God's people on earth, the Lord is king and in control of events in heaven and on earth.

4. Answers will vary. This vision can help us remember that our Lord is the king of the universe and has all events under His control. We might wish that He would use that control to alleviate our suffering, but even if He does not do so immediately, we can be sure that He will be with us in all circumstances, will strengthen us, and will work out all things for our eternal good in Christ.

Closing

Sing or speak together stanzas 1 and 4 of "Immortal, Invisible, God Only Wise."

To Do This Week

Urge participants to read **Ezekiel 1–2** prior to the next session.

Lesson 2

A Watchman

Theme Verse

Invite a volunteer to read aloud the theme verse.

Goal

Read aloud the goal for this lesson.

What's Going On Here?

Read aloud **Ezekiel 2–3.** Then invite volunteers to read aloud the introductory paragraphs.

Searching the Scriptures

1. The phrase *Son of man* is in stark contrast with the transcendence of God, whose glory Ezekiel was privileged to witness. It might have been important for Ezekiel to remember that although he was chosen by God for special service and to witness awesome things, he was still a person, just like those to whom he spoke.

2. **Ezek. 33:21** records the fulfillment of Ezekiel's prophecy that

Jerusalem would fall. No matter how stubbornly the people refused to heed Ezekiel's message, God confirmed the word of His prophet by bringing to pass what he had spoken.

3. Ezekiel, Jeremiah, and John all experienced prophetic inspiration as that of eating, or grasping and digesting fully, the word of the Lord. Ezekiel experienced a sweet taste upon eating as did John. After eating, Jeremiah was filled with inner delight and joy. John found that the bitterness of the message was evident as sourness in his stomach. Although their message was at times bitter, all these prophets found that there is deep joy and satisfaction in internalizing and speaking the word of the Lord. While those who proclaim God's message today no longer receive direct revelation, they must grasp and digest the message of Scripture before they can proclaim it. That proclamation is sometimes bitter in that it involves speaking God's judgment. But that is done in order to bring people to repentance and prepare them for the Gospel. Even amid the bitterness, speaking God's Word provides deep joy.

4. Paul, like Ezekiel, experienced a ministry full of obstacles: weaknesses, insults, hardships, persecutions, and difficulties. But Paul found that those obstacles provided the opportunity for God's strength to work and shine. Paul's experience illustrates that many times Christian ministry is not easy. But like Paul we can rejoice in the obstacles, knowing that through them God's power is displayed as He works through and in spite of them and overcomes them.

5. Moses, Jonah, and Jeremiah all were reluctant to accept the Lord's call whether out of fear of hardship or out of a sense that they were not able to carry out the assignment or both. Although the Bible does not tell us why Ezekiel was troubled in spirit, it could have been a similar reluctance. God chooses whomever He wants, and often He picks those who, by worldly standards, seem unlikely choices. Moses had difficulty speaking, and Jeremiah was only a youth. And He works in those people's lives to equip them and to overcome their reluctance and fear. Paul, a persecutor of God's church, experienced the Lord's call when he was confronted on the road to Damascus by the Lord Jesus. Like Ezekiel, Paul was overwhelmed for several days by his encounter with the Lord.

6. The watchman is responsible to warn people of danger, in this case of the spiritual danger of sin. The watchman is not responsible for whether people accept that warning and repent or reject that warning and die in their sin. In all cases the sinner is responsible for his or her own sin, but the watchman is also accountable for the deaths of those he should have warned and did not. The weight of that responsibility makes the pastoral office more difficult. In addition, although they are not responsible for

whether or not people accept their message, spokespeople for God want to deliver their message in a way that will most likely be received by their hearers. Of course, being sinners, professional church workers will fail at times. For them too the message of forgiveness for Christ's sake is all important.

7. Our responsibility when we speak God's truth is to convey the message accurately, without adding things to it or leaving things out of it. Answers will vary.

The Word for Us

1. We, like all people, were spiritually dead in our sins and needed God to bring us to life, which He has mercifully done in Christ. As a result of that coming to life, we, now in union with Christ, have been raised with Him and seated with Him in the heavenly realms. Like Ezekiel we have been called into God's service; we have been created in Christ to do the good works that God prepared beforehand for us to do.

2. We are "prophets" in the sense that we are called to proclaim God's message to those around us. Unlike Ezekiel we do not receive direct revelation; we share the message recorded in the Bible. Also, most of us are called to witness to individuals rather than to assume spiritual leadership for a group of people. As witnesses, we are called to speak to unrepentant sinners of their sin and of their need for God's forgiveness. And we are called to speak to contrite sinners of the forgiveness, reconciliation, and new life that Christ won for them on the cross.

Closing

Sing or speak together the stanzas printed in the study guide from "Lord of the Living Harvest" as a closing prayer.

To Do This Week

Urge participants to read **Ezekiel 4–5** in preparation for the next lesson.

Lesson 3
A Sign for Israel

Theme Verse
Read aloud the theme verse.

Goal
Invite a volunteer to read aloud the goal statement.

What's Going On Here?
Read aloud or invite a volunteer to read aloud the introductory paragraphs.

Searching the Scriptures

1. In **Ezekiel 13** God condemned the practice of false prophecy and the use of magic charms with which some women had misled His people. The passages from the Pentateuch show how detestable the Lord found occult practices; those who engaged in them were to be put to death. The nations in Canaan were driven out before the Israelites arrived because of such practices.

2. Perhaps the reason God communicated more messages using symbolic actions through Ezekiel than through other prophets was because of the hardness of the people's hearts. If they would not listen to words, perhaps they could be reached by visual messages.

3. The purpose of the acts of Isaiah and Jeremiah was the same as those of Ezekiel: to visually portray something that the Lord was going to cause to happen as judgment for sin. In the **Acts** account, the element of judgment was not present. In that case, the symbolic act showed something that the Lord would allow to happen, not something that He was causing to happen for the punishment of sin.

4. The 430 years might have brought to mind the total number of years that the people of Israel were in Egypt.

5. Answers will vary. Of course the details of the unfaithfulness and idolatry are different in our day, but the underlying sins are the same. Most likely Ezekiel's message would be ignored by most people today as it probably was in his day.

6. The scarcity of food in Jerusalem was so bad that people sold all their belongings to buy food, infants and children suffered and died, and finally people resorted to cannibalism.

7. Ezekiel was appalled that the Lord would instruct him to defile himself. He reminded the Lord how he had kept himself ritually clean all his life. Ezekiel was allowed to cook his food over cow manure instead.

8. Shaving one's hair was a sign of intense mourning. The picture of Ezekiel's shaved hair would communicate to the people that he was in deep mourning because of their sin and the consequences it would bring.

9. The people had rejected the Lord's laws and statues and had acted worse than the surrounding nations. They had engaged in idol worship, defiling the temple with vile images and detestable practices.

10. The Lord would remove His favor from His people and severely punish them for their unfaithfulness, sending famine, plague, and bloodshed to destroy them and make them an object of horror and warning to other nations. Ezekiel's actions with his hair were to symbolize that a third of the people would die of plague or famine within the besieged city, a third would fall by the sword outside the city walls, and a third would be taken into exile and pursued with a drawn sword.

11. The hope in this gloomy picture was that a few people would be spared.

12. The survivors would know that the LORD (Yahweh) is the true God, that He is a jealous God who will not tolerate idolatry, that He was grieved by their unfaithfulness to Him, and that He did not threaten punishment in vain. They would repent of their lustful idolatry and loathsome practices.

The Word for Us

1. Answers will vary. In the passages from **Matthew** both John the Baptist and Jesus talked about how the wrath of God against sin will be expressed in the final judgment when all who have not repented and believed the Gospel will be thrown into eternal fire. The knowledge that God judges sinners and that they are sinners prepares people for the Gospel. Without knowledge of their sinfulness people would see no need for God's gift of forgiveness in Christ.

2. Word pictures give people something to visualize and more readily relate to than does logic. Figurative language is more apt to touch people's hearts as well as their heads. Answers will vary. If your spouse said something that hurt you, which of the following statements might more effectively communicate your feelings? (a) I was really hurt by what you said. (b) When you said that, I felt like my feelings had been run over with a forklift.

As Christian witnesses, we can construct our own word pictures as we share God's message with others, pictures that uniquely fit the situation or the individual to whom we are witnessing. Or we can use the word pictures presented in Scripture. Think of how effectively the parable of the lost sheep **(Luke 15:1–7)** communicates how God seeks the salvation of each of us.

Closing

Pray together the closing prayer.

To Do This Week

Urge participants to read **Ezekiel 6–7** in preparation for the next lesson.

Lesson 4

The Day of Doom

Theme Verse

Read aloud the theme verse.

Goal

Read aloud the goal statement.

What's Going On Here?

Invite a volunteer to read aloud the introductory paragraph.

Searching the Scriptures

1. "The word of the LORD came to me" was the introductory phrase used by Ezekiel. It stressed that his message came from the Lord.

2. The Israelites were commanded even before they entered Canaan to destroy the pagan worship sites, not to worship the Lord in the manner of the Canaanites, and to worship the Lord only in the place that He would designate. These commands were given so that worship of Yahweh would not become corrupted by pagan ideas and practices.

3. The Valley of Ben Hinnom was turned into a site for the worship of Baal, worship that included child sacrifice, a thing unthinkable and totally repugnant to the Lord. Child sacrifice was practiced by the kings Ahaz and Manasseh **(2 Kings 16:2–3; 21:1, 6)**.

4. The Lord would totally destroy the worship sites, the idols, and all the associated objects, desecrating them with human bones. The people would

be killed by sword, famine, and plague and would lie slain among their smashed idols.

5. All the towns would be laid waste, and the entire land from south (the desert) to north (Riblah/Diblah) would be made a desolate waste. In Hebrew the letters r and d look very similar. As some manuscripts indicate, the city mentioned in **6:14** may be Riblah, a city north of Damascus.

6. The survivors would know that Yahweh is the only true God, the all-powerful God who was able to destroy their powerless idols, the Lord of events, the holy God who tolerates no rivals and who punishes apostasy.

7. These survivors would remember that their spiritual adultery grieved the Lord deeply. They would loathe themselves and their detestable ways. In other words, they would repent.

8. In a vision Ezekiel saw the Israelite nation as a group of dried up and scattered bones that the Lord joined together, enfleshed, and brought to life with His Spirit. Ezekiel did not see the resurrection of those who had died but a vision that foretold the restoration of the people to their land. This restoration began when the Persian king Cyrus decreed that any one of God's people who wished could go back to Jerusalem to rebuild the temple.

9. The word *end* occurs five times and the words *come* or *coming* eight times (in the NIV). The words convey urgency and grief. Answers will vary. Of course, we don't know how Ezekiel's hearers reacted, but perhaps some of them caught the sense of inevitability and sorrow in Ezekiel's words and believed his message.

10. God would turn His face from His people and thus remove His blessing, exactly the opposite of the Aaronic benediction. He would allow robbers to come and desecrate His temple. The use of the term "My treasured place" testified to the grief that the Lord felt at the coming destruction.

11. The people were being judged also for social crimes, for violence and bloodshed. God would deal with them according to their conduct. Those who had dealt in violence would be dealt violence in return.

12. Jeremiah's contemporaries assumed that they would always have the teaching of the priests, the word of the prophets, and the advice of those who were wise. Ezekiel prophesied that in the time of the people's dire need no visions would come to the prophets, the teaching of the priests would be lost, as would the counsel of civic leaders. The king would be helpless to do anything but mourn and despair.

The Word for Us

1. Answers will vary. People in their depravity can make anything into a god; examples might include other people, false religions, money, careers,

drugs. Once you understand on what people place their trust, you can begin to point out situations in which those things would utterly fail as did the silver and gold and idols relied on by the people of Ezekiel's day. Point out that God calls sinners to repentance. He offers full and complete forgiveness to all people through faith in Christ Jesus.

2. Trouble can have two effects on people: it can lead them to see the futility of placing their ultimate trust in someone or something other than in God and drive them to God for help, or it can lead them to blame God for the trouble. Because we don't enjoy pain, we usually don't welcome trouble. Yet trouble and the sorrow it brings can result in good. Trouble can lead unbelievers to see their need for God and remind Christians of that need. Christians can embrace the promise of God found in **Romans 8:39:** Nothing "will be able to separate us from the love of God, that is in Christ Jesus our Lord."

Closing

Sing or speak together the stanzas from "Christians, While on Earth Abiding" as a closing prayer.

To Do This Week

Urge participants to read **Ezekiel 8–9** in preparation for the next lesson.

Lesson 5
Visions of Crime and Punishment

Theme Verse

Read aloud the theme verse.

Goal

Invite a volunteer to read aloud the goal for this lesson.

What's Going On Here?

Invite participants to read aloud these introductory paragraphs.

Searching the Scriptures

1. In the temple, the sanctuary of the Lord, Ezekiel was shown the glory of the Lord as he had seen it near the Kebar River. In sharp contrast,

Ezekiel also saw something that did not belong in the temple of the living God, an idol. Although the diagram of the temple in lesson 11 is of the temple Ezekiel saw in a vision, it had much the same layout as the temple in Jerusalem. You might want to consult it to locate the place to which Ezekiel was transported in his vision.

2. The Lord had warned His people on Mt. Sinai that He is a jealous God who rightly will not tolerate idolatry. He had chosen the temple in Jerusalem as the special dwelling place for His name, and it had been corrupted by the worship of false gods, who were really no gods at all. The idol that Ezekiel saw may have been an Asherah pole like the one Manasseh placed in the temple. In Canaanite mythology, Asherah was the consort of Baal. Asherah poles were probably wooden representations of her.

3. Such detestable practices would drive the Lord far from His sanctuary.

4. The sin committed by the elders was grievous because it involved the worship of images made in the likeness of created things.

5. The elders assumed that the Lord did not see what they were doing and that He had forsaken the land. They denied both His omniscience—that He knows everything—and His omnipresence—that He is present everywhere at all times.

6. The worship of Tammuz denied the Lord's creation and control over the seasons, the rains, and the growth of vegetation. The worship of Tammuz was a direct violation of the commandment not to have other gods before Yahweh.

7. The Lord had warned His people not to be enticed to worship the sun, moon, and stars, which He had created for the benefit of all nations.

8. The glory of the Lord moved from above the cherubim to the threshold of the temple. This could refer to one of two things; (a) The living cherubim that propelled the Lord's throne are meant. In that case the glory moved from the throne to the threshold. (b) The cherubim referred to are those on the mercy seat of the ark of the covenant in the Most Holy Place. It was between these cherubim that the glory had resided since the dedication of the temple. In that case, this movement from above the cherubim to the threshold began the exodus of the Lord's glory from the temple that would precede its destruction.

9. "The soul who sins is the one who will die."

10. In **Rev. 19:7–8** linen stands for the righteous acts of the saints. The idea of the purity of fine linen probably underlies its use in all of the verses listed.

11. The servants of God will have a mark placed on their forehead. The mark means that they belong to God. It will protect them from the coming judgments as foretold in **Revelation.** Point out that we by God's grace

through faith in Jesus have been marked with God's righteousness.

12. Ezekiel acted in the role of a mediator, pleading to the Lord for the people. The Lord responded that the sin of Israel and Judah was exceedingly great and would be punished.

13. The man clad in linen had finished his errand; those who were faithful to the Lord had been spared.

The Word for Us

1. That God repeatedly addressed people's rejection of Him throughout Scripture shows that He does see and care when people turn their backs on Him. Those who do so act foolishly, exchanging God for something created and worthless. They will be turned to shame and will experience God's wrath. We, too, should take that warning to heart lest we turn our backs on Him and rely on something other than Him to sustain our spiritual life.

2. Belief in astrology is antithetical to belief in the true God. Casual use of astrology by Christians gives the impression that it is compatible with Christianity, which it is not. Casual use by anyone indicates a dangerous indifference to the lure astrology can have on people. Answers will vary. To those who trust in such things, we can witness to the fact that the Lord created the heavenly bodies and point out the foolishness of relying on something created rather than on the Creator. For those who confess their sin, we share the forgiveness of sin Christ Jesus won for us on the cross.

3. **Matt. 6:24** warns against serving money, and **Phil. 3:19** notes the preoccupation of some people with earthly things, including fulfilling their appetites and desires. Answers will vary. Immersion in the Word of God, regular use of the sacraments, prayer, Christian literature, being accountable to other Christians, and their prayers and counsel are effective in helping Christians remain faithful to the Lord. The Lord Himself working through Word and Sacrament strengthens our faith and enables us to remain faithful.

Closing

Read or sing together stanzas 1 and 2 of "From God Can Nothing Move Me" as a closing prayer.

To Do This Week

Urge participants to read **Ezekiel 10–11** in preparation for the next lesson.

Lesson 6
Jerusalem Burned and Forsaken

Theme Verse
Read aloud the theme verse.

Goal
Invite a volunteer to read aloud the goal for this lesson.

What's Going On Here?
Read aloud the introductory paragraph.

Searching the Scriptures

1. The Lord commanded the man in linen to take some of the burning coals from among the cherubim and scatter them over the city. Several years after Ezekiel's vision (in 586 B.C.), the Babylonians burned all the important buildings of Jerusalem, including the temple. Ezekiel's vision emphasized that the Babylonians were but the agents of God.

2. The glory of the Lord left the threshold and mounted the throne above the cherubim. The cherubim, with the glory of the Lord above them, then rose from the ground and halted at the entrance to the east gate of the temple. The temple is called the Lord's house.

3. The people assumed that the Lord would never allow His house to be destroyed. They felt that no matter how they lived they were safe because the Lord had placed His name on the temple. Jeremiah proclaimed that the Lord would act in response to His people's unfaithfulness and the temple would not stop the coming judgment; only their repentance could do that. Ezekiel was shown this vision of the Lord departing from the temple and thereby leaving it open to destruction.

4. The Spirit of the Lord led Ezekiel to prophesy that the bodies of the innocent killed in the city would be the protected meat and that the living people in the city would be driven out and handed over to foreigners who would inflict punishment on them by killing them with the sword. Then the people who had not followed Yahweh's decrees but had instead conformed to the standards of the surrounding nations would know that He is the Lord.

5. To those who had been driven far from the sanctuary of the Lord, the Lord Himself would be a sanctuary in a foreign land. The Lord promised to gather them from all the nations where they had been scattered and to

bring them back to the land of Israel.

6. The Lord would give the returnees an undivided heart that would serve Him only. He would remove their cold, stony heart that was unresponsive to Him and give them a heart of flesh. Then they would keep His decrees and laws and remove all the detestable idols from the land. The Lord restated the heart of His covenant with the descendants of Abraham that He would be their God and they would be His people.

7. The Lord would bring down upon those who were unfaithful to Him the punishment that they deserved.

8. The glory of the Lord above the cherubim went up from within the city and stopped above the Mount of Olives, east of the city. This meant that the Lord was abandoning His city to destruction.

9. Ezekiel told everything that the Lord had shown him to the exiles.

The Word for Us

1. Scoffers ridicule the idea that Jesus will come again as He promised to bring this world to an end. They say that things will continue with the world as they have since creation. Jesus is patient, not wanting any to perish but all to repent, and He is giving them time to do so. As we await His coming, we should live holy and godly lives. We look forward to the new heavens and new earth—the home of righteousness—that His coming will bring.

2. With the mighty power of God, the Holy Spirit works in our hearts that Christ might dwell there through faith. The Spirit enables us to grasp the enormous love of Christ that we might be filled with God's fullness, rooted and established in His love. The result of that work is that we crucify our sinful nature and live lives worthy of our calling—lives characterized by humbleness, patience, gentleness, forbearance in love, unity, joy, peace, kindness, goodness, faithfulness, and self-control.

Closing

Sing or speak together stanzas 3 and 4 of "Renew Me, O Eternal Light" as a closing prayer.

To Do This Week

Urge participants to read the suggested chapters of **Ezekiel** prior to the next session.

Lesson 7
Ezekiel, Prophet of Restoration

Theme Verse
Read aloud the theme verse.

Goal
Invite a volunteer to read aloud the goal statement.

What's Going On Here?
Invite volunteers to read aloud these introductory paragraphs.

Searching the Scriptures

1. When the Lord told Ezekiel to warn a wicked man that he would die unless he repented, Ezekiel was responsible for passing along the warning. The individual then was responsible for heeding the message. If he heeded the message and turned from his wicked ways he would live. If he did not repent he would die. The prophet who warned him would bear no responsibility.

2. When Ezekiel's hearers finally acknowledged their sin, they exhibited a fatalistic attitude and stoically resigned themselves to wasting away because of that sin.

3. Ezekiel was called to proclaim to these people that the Lord took no pleasure in the death of the wicked, but rather that He took pleasure when they turned from their wicked ways (repented) and lived. The Lord's declaration began with this divine oath: "As surely as I live." Nothing is more sure. The Lord wants all people to have the full benefits of life as He intended it to be lived now and throughout eternity.

4. The righteous person who turned to evil would not be allowed to live on the basis of his or her former righteousness but would die because of his or her sin.

5. The Lord would forgive the repentant person, no longer counting against that person his or her former sins. That person would live. Through the power of the Holy Spirit, a repentant person lives a God-pleasing life in conformity with the will and law of God (33:14–15).

6. The word of judgment indicated by Ezekiel's dumbness was that the people were so rebellious that the Lord withheld His word from them except at certain times.

7. The removal of Ezekiel's dumbness indicated that the Lord's judgment

on the city, of which Ezekiel up to that time had warned, had been carried out. Now Ezekiel would be able to proclaim the Lord's word unhindered.

8. The sins of the survivors were no different than the sins for which the Lord brought judgment on the land. Ezekiel was called to proclaim that they too would die for their sin and that the Lord would make the land a desolate waste, thus cleansing it from all those who engaged in detestable practices.

9. Ezekiel's fellow exiles did not put his words into practice. Although they claimed to be devoted to the Lord, their hearts were preoccupied with unjust gain.

10. The people would finally take Ezekiel seriously as a prophet of the Lord when what he said came to pass.

The Word for Us

1. The person who takes the Word of the Lord seriously puts it into practice. Those who do so build their lives on a solid foundation that will support them no matter what the devil or the world throw against them. Those who do not put the Word of the Lord into practice have built their lives on an unstable foundation that will collapse and ultimately destroy them. Note that putting the Word into practice involves trusting in the Lord as well as living lives of love and obedience (see **John 6:28–29**). Answers will vary. Our sinful nature always wants to lead us into disregarding the Lord's Word and going after the unjust gain offered by the world. The power and motivation to put the Word into practice come from God as the Holy Spirit works through that very same Word and through the sacraments.

2. The Lord rejoices when sinners repent. The Pharisees and teachers of the law muttered against Jesus for eating with tax collectors and "sinners." Jesus told the parables in **Luke 15** that they might repent of their sinful attitude. Reactions such as those of the Pharisees and teachers of the law stem from such things as arrogance and jealousy. Answers will vary. We should always remember that we too are sinners and deserve from God nothing but punishment but that He instead has saved us by His grace in Christ. That will enable us to rejoice with God when others repent and receive His forgiveness.

Closing

Pray together the closing prayer.

To Do This Week

Urge participants to read **Ezekiel 34** in preparation for the next lesson.

Lesson 8

The Shepherd-King

Theme Verse

Read aloud the theme verse.

Goal

Invite a volunteer to read aloud the goal statement.

What's Going On Here?

Invite volunteers to read aloud this rather lengthy introductory section.

Searching the Scriptures

1. Using language about shepherds and their flocks, the Lord accused the religious and civil leaders of having used those under their care for their own selfish ends.

2. These leaders failed to carry out their responsibility to look after those who were weak and hurting and lost. Not only did they neglect those duties, but they ruled the people with harshness.

3. The result of this bad leadership was that the people of Israel were scattered among the nations, easy prey for those who would devour them.

4. In Jesus' day also, God's people lacked good leadership and so were harassed and helpless.

5. The Israelites were the people the Lord had chosen out of all the people of the world to be His treasured possession, a kingdom of priests and a holy nation. They were the flock under His care.

6. Kings, prophets, and priests were consecrated as God's representatives by being anointed with oil. This anointing indicated that they were being set apart for God's service.

7. The Lord Himself would search for His sheep, gather them from all the places where they were scattered, bring them back to their own land, and there richly provide for them. The Lord Himself would look after the weak and sick and lost. But the sleek and strong He would destroy. Justice would prevail in His dealings with His people.

8. The strong and powerful not only used the best provisions, they spoiled what they did not use, so that the weak were left with what they had mauled.

9. Jesus, the Good Shepherd, would lay down His life for the sheep and gather all of His sheep into one flock. This Shepherd-Prince will rule forever. All of the passages listed are messianic promises in which the Lord

promised to raise up a ruler from the line of David. His reign will be characterized by justice and righteousness.

10. The passages listed point forward to the perfect bliss and harmony that we will experience fully in heaven. Answers will vary. Jesus' blood shed on the cross purchased our redemption, the forgiveness of our sins, and thus made possible peace between people and God, who had been enemies because of sin.

The Word for Us

1. Jesus' sheep, those who believe in Him, are incorporated into a unity like that shared by the Father and the Son. The sheep share the same faith in Jesus as their Savior, Shepherd, and King. This is not a new-age unity that obliterates individual personalities and merges all into a "god consciousness." It is instead a unity of faith, of love, and of purpose. We became members of the flock through faith in Jesus. Jesus assures us that He has given us eternal life and no one will be able to snatch us out of His hand or the Father's hand.

2. Pastors are to shepherd God's flock by serving them, not lording it over them, but by being examples to them. Answers will vary. Scripture calls upon us to obey our pastors and to imitate their way of life and their faith. Of course this is not to be done blindly. Pastors too are sinful, and if they are leading us into sin, of course we must obey God rather than them (see **Acts 4:18–20**). We are also to pray for our pastors and their task of proclaiming the Gospel. Other suggestions might include having realistic expectations and giving the pastor time to do his job as the shepherd of souls rather than expecting him to be an administrator or a financial manager or to attend every meeting. We support our pastor when we encourage and allow him to spend time with his family. And we owe to our pastor the consideration we owe to everyone, not to criticize him or gossip about him. The words of Luther apply also to how we treat our pastor: "We should fear and love God so that we do not tell lies about our neighbor, betray him, slander him, or hurt his reputation, but defend him, speak well of him, and explain everything in the kindest way" (Small Catechism, explanation of the Eighth Commandment).

Closing

Sing or speak together "The Lord's My Shepherd, I'll Not Want" as the closing prayer.

To Do This Week

Urge participants to read **Ezekiel 35–37** in preparation for the next session.

Lesson 9
Restoration to Life

Theme Verse
Read aloud or invite a volunteer to read aloud the theme verse.

Goal
Read aloud the goal statement.

What's Going On Here?
Invite volunteers to read aloud the introductory paragraphs.

Searching the Scriptures

1. Ezekiel saw a great number of bones. The bones were very dry indicating that the people had been dead for a very long time. The Lord asked Ezekiel if the bones could live. Ezekiel replied that the Lord alone knew. It would have seemed unlikely for dry bones to come to life.

2. The word of the Lord as prophesied by Ezekiel caused the bones to come together, covered them with tendons and flesh and skin, and gave them the breath of life. The two-step process recalled the creation of Adam.

3. The people were described as a vast army.

4. The dry bones represented the whole house of Israel, whose hopes for survival appeared dead and buried in the exile. Prospects of national survival were as bleak as it was unlikely for a vast array of skeletons, dismembered and dried, again to pulsate with life. The coming to life of the bones represented the return of God's people back to their land. This could only be accomplished at the Lord's command, just as dry bones could only come to life at His command.

5. The people would know that Yahweh is the Lord. Only He could reverse such a hopeless situation and bring His people from the death of exile to life in their own land. The Lord promised to give His people His life-giving Spirit as they returned to their land.

Read aloud and discuss the lengthy section on interpreting prophesy.

6. In binding together of the two sticks of wood representing the kingdoms of Israel and Judah, Ezekiel was prophesying that in the messianic age, God's people will be united. Gone will be the hostility that divided God's people into two nations after Solomon. The messianic age is likened to the golden age of Israel under David, before it was divided and it fell into idolatry.

7. God's people will no longer defile themselves with idolatry. God will cleanse them and save them from their sinful backsliding. Then He will be their God and they will be His people. The Messiah will be their king forever. They will be careful to follow God's laws. They and their children will live in the land of Israel forever. God will make an everlasting covenant of peace with His people. He will establish them and cause their numbers to increase. God will put His sanctuary among them forever and dwell with them. When the Lord's sanctuary is among His people, then the nations will know that the Lord is the one who makes His people holy.

8. The idea that God's people would live forever in the land of Israel belonged to Ezekiel's time and not to the essence of the prophecy.

9. The messianic era prophesied by Ezekiel began with the coming of Jesus the Messiah but will not be consummated until Jesus returns again to bring this world to an end and to call all of His servants to live with Him and the Father forever in the new heavens and new earth. Answers may vary. The following are ways in which the fulfillment of Ezekiel's prophecy is/will be greater than what he predicted: The Messiah is not only a son of David, but also the Son of God. The new covenant has been sealed with the blood of the Messiah, which was poured out for the forgiveness of sins. The Messiah's kingdom is not of this world; it is a spiritual kingdom that transcends national and earthly boundaries. The blood of the Messiah purchased servants of God from all peoples of the earth, not just the people of Israel. In the new heavens and the new earth there will be no more pain or sorrow. The Lord God Almighty and the Lamb (Jesus) will be the sanctuary (temple), so a building for God's dwelling will be unnecessary.

The Word for Us

1. Using a wordplay, Jesus likened the work of the Holy Spirit in bringing about the rebirth of people to the blowing of the wind. Like the wind, which blows where it pleases, the Spirit's work is unseen by us and beyond our comprehension, yet we see evidence of it. Answers will vary. In your discussion stress the Holy Spirit's work in bringing us to new life in Christ and keeping us in that life that will never end.

2. Both the prophets Elijah and Elisha prayed to the Lord to raise a boy from the dead and the Lord answered their prayer by doing so. The other passages declare what is clearer in the New Testament: that the Lord will redeem His people from death and take them to be with Him in glory forever. Answers will vary. Just as it is God who gives life in the first place, so God can raise people to life after they die. This power of God over death raised our Lord Jesus from the dead. His resurrection assures us that we too will be raised to new life, life with Him that will last for eternity.

Closing

Sing or speak together stanzas 1 and 4 of "To God the Holy Spirit Let Us Pray."

To Do This Week

Urge participants to read **Ezekiel 38–39** prior to the next session.

Lesson 10

Restoration to Safety

Theme Verse

Invite a volunteer to read aloud the theme verse.

Goal

Read aloud the goal statement.

What's Going On Here?

Invite a volunteer to read aloud the introductory paragraph.

Searching the Scriptures

1. Ezekiel was instructed to prophesy that the Lord was against Gog and would turn him around, put hooks in his jaws, and bring him and his vast hordes out. The defeat of God's enemies is absolutely assured even before they formulate their plans.

2. God's people are described as having been gathered from exile and living in safety in the land of Israel. They are peaceful and unsuspecting, living in villages without walls, bars, or gates. Their defenselessness would seem to indicate that they rely on the Lord alone as their defense.

3. Gog would plan to attack this seemingly defenseless people and loot them of all their riches. The sense of **38:13** seems to be that other nations would greedily want to share in the plunder.

4. These events would take place "after many days" and "in future years." Gog and his forces would be so numerous that they would seem like a cloud covering the land.

5. Gog would devise the evil scheme, but God would use that scheme for His purposes. This

does not mean that Gog is a luckless pawn in the hand of an all-powerful but immoral God. Gog freely acts according to the evil dictates of his lust for conquest and easy spoil, but behind everything in the universe (and especially as it relates to God's people) there is the controlling hand of God, who orders all things with a view to the ultimate vindication of His honour among the nations. What Gog imagines to be a victory for himself, the Lord turns into an opportunity for His glory (John B. Taylor, *Ezekiel: An Introduction and Commentary* [Downers Grove, IL: Inter-Varsity Press, 1969], p. 246).

The Lord's purpose would be that through the defeat of Gog, the Lord would be shown to be the one true, holy God in the sight of the nations.

6. At Gog's invasion, the Lord's hot anger would be kindled.

7. The Lord Himself would fight for Israel using a great earthquake, plague, bloodshed, torrents of rain, hailstones, and burning sulfur. Throughout Scripture, these elements are associated with God's judgment. Gog's hordes would fight against each other in a panic.

8. The Lord had spoken; it would surely happen as He has said.

9. Gog and his army would be disarmed by God before they could fight. Their bodies would be food for birds and wild animals. God would send fire against their homeland. The people of Israel would use their weapons for fuel for seven years. For seven months, people would be engaged in burying their bodies. The number *seven* emphasizes the completeness of the defeat.

10. Such a graphic description communicates how terrible is the judgment of the Lord. Unless people realize how terrible it is, they will not fear it. Fearing God's judgment can lead people to repentance.

11. Israel would know that Yahweh is their God. The nations would know that Israel went into exile because of the people's sin not because of the Lord's weakness.

12. The Lord would have compassion on all His people and be zealous for His holy name.

13. God's promise to no longer hide His face from His people means that the Lord's face would be turned toward them in blessing. The promise of His Spirit would enable them to be the people He desired them to be.

The Word for Us

1. **Ezekiel 38–39** proclaims that the Lord is in control of all events, even those that seem the darkest and the most fearsome. Although God's people may seem defenseless, the Lord Himself will fight for them and will win the ultimate victory over the forces of evil. This message can comfort us in our dark hours, just as it comforted God's Old Testament people in their dark hour of exile.

2. Jesus said that only the Father knows the hour of Jesus' return and that it is not for His disciples to know the time that the Father has appointed. As we await Jesus' return, we are to be watchful, expecting His return at any time. We are to be faithful stewards, working at the tasks He has given us. We are to be His witnesses, proclaiming the Gospel throughout the world.

Closing

Sing or speak together "Do Not Despair, O Little Flock" as a closing prayer.

To Do This Week

Urge participants to skim **Ezekiel 40–48** to prepare for Lesson 11.

Lesson 11

"The LORD Is There"

Theme Verse

Read aloud or invite a volunteer to read aloud the theme verse.

Goal

Invite a volunteer to read aloud the goal statement.

What's Going On Here?

Read aloud or invite a volunteer to read aloud the introductory paragraph.

Searching the Scriptures

1. The man told Ezekiel to pay close attention to what he was seeing because he was to tell everything he saw to the house of Israel.

2. The temple, as well as the entire complex, had a foursquare symmetry and a balanced completeness in its structure, symbolic of the perfection of a holy habitation of the Lord.

3. Ezekiel's vision of the return of the Lord's glory to the temple meant that God would once again dwell among His people.

4. The Lord promised that this dwelling place would be where He would live among His people forever and that the people would never again defile His holy name.

5. Ezekiel's description was meant to invoke shame in the people because of their sins. They were to put away their idols that the Lord might dwell among them.

6. Ezekiel's prophecy will be completely fulfilled at the end of this age, in the new heaven and new earth, where God will dwell directly with His people.

7. Jesus, our great High Priest, offered His blood as the sacrifice that procured atonement for all people, once and for all.

8. The source of the river seen by Ezekiel in his vision was the temple, where the presence of God dwelt. The river would have healing and life-nurturing properties. Where it flowed into the Dead Sea, it would make the salt water fresh, thus making possible the life of plants and animals. Its waters would nourish the life of many fruit trees, which would bear fruit every month. This fruit would be good for food and for healing. The river symbolizes the blessings of life and healing that flow from the Lord's presence.

9. In heaven we will fully enjoy the blessings of the water of life because then we will be directly in the presence of God.

10. Ezekiel's vision dealt with the return of the Lord to dwell among His people and what that would mean for them. The name of the city summarizes this all-important theme: the presence of God with His people. In the beginning of his ministry, Ezekiel was called to proclaim to the people that the Lord could no longer dwell in their midst because of their divided loyalty, their unfaithfulness to Him with other gods. In a vision, Ezekiel saw the withdrawal of the Lord's glory from the temple and the city. But after their destruction, Ezekiel was called to proclaim that the Lord would cleanse His people from their idolatry and make it possible for them to enjoy full fellowship with Him forever. Thus the name of the city is a fitting ending to **Ezekiel** because it reveals the essence of God's message through Ezekiel: that the Lord desires to dwell among His people and bless them with His presence. In **Revelation 21** John also saw a similar finale to his vision: he saw the coming of the heavenly Jerusalem, where God will make His dwelling directly among His people and will bless them forever.

The Word for Us

1. In **Is. 55:10–11** God promises that His Word will accomplish the purpose for which He sent it. Answers will vary. When times are difficult and it seems like the Lord is responding slowly to our prayers, we can cling to His promise to always be with us **(Heb. 13:5–6)** and His promise that in all things He works for our eternal good in Christ **(Rom. 8:28).** We can see from Ezekiel that God works in ways that far surpass our expectations even as He sometimes seems to work slowly. For instance, Ezekiel's

promise of God's dwelling among His people will be fulfilled in heaven in a far greater way than it would have been in just an earthly temple. We can be certain that God will act according to His promises because He has done so in the past, most notably in sending our Savior, Jesus Christ, whose coming had been promised since the fall into sin **(Gen. 3:15)**.

2. In **1 Cor. 3:16** Paul says that the church (*you* plural) is the temple of God. Therefore, people should be careful not to destroy this temple with quarrels and factions. In **1 Cor. 6:19** Paul can say that our bodies are the temple of the Holy Spirit because the Holy Spirit lives in us, just as God dwelled in the Old Testament temple. In the context Paul is talking about how we should respect the temples of our bodies by fleeing sexual immorality. Since our bodies are the Holy Spirit's temple, we should avoid everything that is destructive of the body. Paul calls us to honor God with our bodies **(v. 20)**.

Closing

Read responsively the selected verses from **Revelation 22** as a closing prayer.

Real lives facing real frustrations need Connections to God and to one another.

The **Connections** Bible study series helps take the concerns of your heart and turn them over to Jesus in worship, prayer, Bible study and discussion.

Connections uses a Gospel-centered message to build trust in God and to develop trusting and supportive relationships with one another, just as Christ intended.

Connections studies look at small portions of Scripture that really hit home, in areas where anxiety is often deepest.

For small groups or individual study, **Connections** uses God's Word to build relationships and bring peace to troubled hearts.

Ask for **Connections** at your Christian bookstore or call CPH, 1 800 325 3040

H54821

3558 SOUTH JEFFERSON AVENUE
SAINT LOUIS MISSOURI 63118-3968

FAMILY

ISSUES

LEARN BIBLICAL PRINCIPLES TO STRENGTHEN AND SUPPORT YOUR FAMILY.

Many trends in our society today threaten the well being of the family. The new Family Life Issues series is designed to respond to these trends by giving identity, strength and direction to families through the study of God's Word.

Find encouragement for your family in this Bible study series that teaches practical skills and gives insight to build homes dedicated to Christ.

Each study contains four sessions.

Growing As a Christian Father
Overcoming Dysfunction
Growing As a Blended Family
Maximizing Media
Growing As a Christian Mother
Growing As a Single Parent
Managing Finances
Life in the Sandwich Generation

CPH

3558 SOUTH JEFFERSON AVENUE
SAINT LOUIS MISSOURI 63118-3968

H55277